THE PLAYERS' BOX

THE PLAYERS' BOX

Tennis Coaching That Shaped The Game

Alex Leslie

Thank you to my partner, Cecilia Madrid, for your unwavering support in helping this book come to life. I couldn't have done it without you.

Contents

Introduction

*"Tennis is an addiction that once it has truly
hooked a man will not let him go".*

Rod Laver

YOU HAVE PROBABLY SEEN IT. It happens all the time.
Whether it's rookies in their first year on the ATP Tour,
or seasoned veterans like Andy Murray or Novak Djokovic.
A tennis player looking over at the players' box throughout
a Grand Slam and yelling in anger after missing that ever so
reliable ground stroke is not something out of the ordinary.
Or in contrast, roaring in delight after winning a big point or
match.

The players' box is primarily for people in an athlete's close
circle, or 'entourage', to sit and watch. Whether that be family,

sponsors, or even Tiger Woods if you're Roger Federer - Tiger's stony visage in the players' box during Federer's Wimbledon triumph in 2012 is probably as iconic as it gets. Greatness admiring greatness.

Despite all the glitz and glamour that can often be observed however, the most important person of all can usually be found in the players' box. Perhaps not as recognisable as some of the players' partners or famous friends, but without doubt the most necessary. The coach. With the rules made crystal clear, coaches are often rendered useless whilst matches are taking place, as any form of coaching when the game is underway is against the rules. Nevertheless, you'll often see the coach sat poker faced, but completely engrossed, absorbing every shot, every movement, and usually facing the brunt of their player's anger when things aren't going their way.

But how important are coaches to tennis players? If they aren't useful in a time of need during a match, perhaps in a final set tie-break when some tactical advice would be greatly beneficial, then why are they needed at all? Imagine the great Sir Alex Ferguson, unable to encourage his players from the side of the pitch during Manchester United's title winning seasons. It's hard to picture Roger Mayweather prohibited from giving his nephew, Floyd, tips and advice in between rounds of his highly illustrious boxing career. The same cannot be said for tennis coaching. All the work is done in private, away from the main event. There are no inspiring charismatic half-time team talks or innovative tactical guidance midway through a set of a tennis match.

If you look closely however, the impact a tennis coach can have on a player is profound. Whether it's Peter Carter's calming influence on a young Roger Federer, or the great personal relationship between former world number one Pete Sampras and Tim Gullikson. A tennis coach is often more than just an individual who helps enhance a player's tennis game, but instead, somebody who aims to improve a player as an athlete and person. Marian Vajda's influence on Novak Djokovic's diet was so profound, Novak has even released a book on diet and nutrition, offering a 14-day gluten-free plan for physical and mental excellence.

This book aims to identify the influence of a tennis coach on their player. Focusing on the best players of the past twenty years, we will peek into the minds of the coaches that helped shape the game. Whether you are a coach at club level, county level, or international level, identifying what makes a great coach tick can certainly help you get the best out of a player.

The Road To The Millennium

The wholesale and widespread changes to the game of tennis since the early 1900s have been rather dramatic. We now see better balls, advanced racquets, and beautifully efficient techniques. But to fully understand and appreciate the game and how far it has come, both in terms of coaching and playing, it's important we delve back in time to the 11th century.

Despite there being sparse evidence in ancient Egypt, Greece and Rome of an early type of tennis, it is the belief of many historians that 11th century French monks discovered and invented the game.[1]

It began with a 'game of the hand', or 'jeu de paume' to its natives. The game, somewhat bizarrely, immediately took the life of its first victim, King Louis X. It is said that after a very exciting but exhausting game of jeu de paume at Château de Vincennes, King Louis X sat down and enjoyed a chilled bottle of wine, subsequently dying of pneumonia not long after.[2] Not the greatest advert for the sport we all know and love today! Nevertheless, this didn't deter players from the game, and it rose in popularity up and down the country.[1] King Louis X is often credited as being the first person to establish indoor tennis courts in the style we know today, and is widely remembered as the first ever tennis player known by name. So, what better way to bow out, right?

Originally, research has shown how courtyard playing areas were transformed into indoor courts, with players hitting the ball with their bare hands against a wall, much to their pain and anguish.[2] It wasn't until the 16th century that a racquet was first introduced, the first time the sport bared any resemblance to today's game.[1] Before that, the game had seen advancement from bare hands to gloves, followed by a solid paddle, but never before had anybody used something that resembled a racquet. The game was on the rise, and when Walter Wingfield, a British army officer, introduced the game to the masses in 1874, the sport never looked back. Wingfield created a 'box set' that was easily accessible for everybody, including rubber balls, a net and court markers for anybody to pick up and make their own makeshift court, along with an instruction manual. Wingfield is credited as being the 'Father' of lawn tennis, and his influence on the sport shouldn't be undermined. Shortly after the release of his 'box sets', you could find tennis courts around the world, in Russia, Canada, the U.S. and India to name a few.[1]

It wasn't long before the first Davis Cup tournament was held in 1900 and within less than twenty years, the four Grand Slams that we all watch and enjoy today were formed: Wimbledon, the U.S. Open, the Australian Open and the French Open. Grand Slam tournaments opened the door for genuine tennis superstars to emerge. Stars like the fashionable Fred Perry, whose dominance in the 1930s was talked about just as much as his off-court romances. Who can forget Roy Emerson's remarkable supremacy of the 1960s, propelling him into international stardom. How about Steffi Graff, the only player to have completed the 'Golden Slam' in the same year, winning all four Grand Slams and Olympic gold in 1988 - a record that doesn't look set to be broken anytime soon. The 80s also produced the somewhat outrageous rivalry between John McEnroe and Bjorn Borg, which will always remain carved in the history books - two incredibly talented players whose personalities shone through into their game: "it was on the line!". Tennis was regularly producing sporting legends.

This book will start at the beginning of the millennium, a year that proved remarkably eventful. Michael Schumacher won his very first Formula One World Championship with Ferrari, Craig David topped UK music charts with his single 'Walking Away', and Big Brother first launched onto our television screens, changing reality TV forever. The game of tennis, too, was also embarking on a radical change.

One could argue that the 90s was an era of the big serve and volley, and the 2000s an era defined by power and brilliant baseline play. They could have a very reasonable argument. The evidence certainly points in that direction, as the only 'baseline' player to win Wimbledon during the 90s was Andre Agassi, who stormed to success in 1992. Perhaps other great 90s baseline players, stars like Jim Courier and Malavai Washington, were slightly ahead of their time. What most champion tennis players looked like twenty-five years ago is vastly different to the attributes that make up a modern day tennis superstar.

The Wimbledon final of 1994 was a prime example of what tennis matches often looked like in the 90s. Pete Sampras and the 6"4 Croat Goran Ivanisevic battled it out on an unusually warm summer's day in the English capital. Those inside Wimbledon's centre court witnessed two big servers regularly hitting speeds of 125-135 mph throughout the match, with little to no baseline rallies to note. The match stats tell you the story, with Ivanisevic firing a huge thirty-two aces over the course of the final. The negative uproar from the media after the match proved important. "The game was too fast and too serve dominated", fans cried.[3] Many believe that the final between Sampras and Ivanisevic was significant in the switch in playing style of players, with the contest even being labelled "the match that changed tennis".[3] I mean, who can blame the fans for being a little perturbed that day. Watching Novak Djokovic and Roger Federer gracefully fire shots from the back of the court is far more aesthetically pleasing. As good a server Goran Ivanisevic and other 90s players were, the game of tennis can't be witnessed in its truest beauty when there is a lack of elegant ground strokes. The drastic change the sport oversaw cannot be pinpointed to just fan uproar however, with a variety of factors to be taken into consideration.

The late 90s witnessed several developments in the game which helped towards the shift to a more baseline dominated approach by the turn of the millennium.[3] Ever advancing technology resulted in huge improvements to player racquets and strings, with newer racquets far more flexible and strung at lower tensions, yielding more control and precision for its owner. After the disappointment of the 1994 Wimbledon final, surfaces of courts were even altered, with the Wimbledon grass slowed to encourage longer rallies.[3]

Perhaps the most eye-catching development started to occur in the women's game. The rise and dominance of power players like Lindsay Davenport, Mary Pierce and of course the fantastic Williams sisters set the tone for women's tennis going forward, and perfectly fit the direction in which tennis was heading. This new style of play made it far more difficult for players like Martina Hingis to dominate, with her attacking net play inefficient against the new, stronger, and more athletic breed of tennis player. Martina's failure to win a major tournament after the year 2000, despite winning five Grand Slams pre-millennium, is a case in point. Whilst in no doubt still a very good player, the game had simply moved on.

The 2002 Wimbledon final between Hewitt and Nalbandian was a clear inflection point. It signalled the end of an era, and the start of an incredibly promising one. For the first time, two young, athletic and hard hitting baseline players were battling it out to become Wimbledon's new king. In hindsight, it should have come as no surprise. Players who relied heavily on their serving and volleying were being outplayed. Their movement wasn't as smooth and their ground strokes were suspect when pitted against the modern player.

All these factors were the catalyst for the game of tennis to head towards a new explosive direction, and it is here where we begin the first chapter.

Chapter One

Pete Sampras & Tim Gullikson

"I never wanted to be the great guy or the colourful guy or the interesting guy. I wanted to be the guy that won titles".

Pete Sampras

IT'S JULY 9TH 2000, and where better to start the journey of this book than with the brilliant Pete Sampras. It was a year that witnessed the American prodigy win his 13th Grand Slam title, with the world of tennis in awe as they watched him lift the Wimbledon trophy for the 7th and final time. An unprecedented achievement, and a record that remained unbroken until a certain Mr Roger Federer came along.

The Wimbledon Championships that year saw a special celebration. All living champions, two time finalists, and players who had won four or more doubles titles were invited back to SW19 as part of a special ceremony to mark the turn of the millennium. Each honouree was handed a crystal plate perfectly engraved with their name on, awarded by Her Royal Highness, The Duchess of Gloucester.

The start of the tournament, however, did not start well for Sampras. The American had developed inflammation after pulling a muscle in his shin and seemingly had no idea how it happened. The pain was so unpleasant, he had even considered pulling out of the tournament completely. "I played and won my second round match against Karol Kucera, and in that match I felt pain every time I put weight on my right foot", Sampras recalled.[4] At the time, Sampras was level with Roy Emerson for the most Grand Slam title victories, with both men boasting 12 each. Pulling out simply wasn't a realistic or viable option, with breaking the record and claiming his 13th at the forefront of his mind. To ease some of the discomfort, he decided not to practice in between matches. "After my second round match, I no longer practiced on my off days. I went out for every match without having hit a ball in practice. That made me uneasy and the constant pain was wearing on me".[4] Sampras' route to the Wimbledon final that year consisted of Justin Gimlestob in the third round, followed by Jonas

Bjorkman, Jan-Michael Gambill, and Belorussian qualifier Vladimir Voltchkov. A relatively easy draw on paper, but matches relentlessly filled with pain and anguish.[4]

Through sheer grit and determination, aligned with regular shots of cortisone, Sampras made it to the final, where he would face the popular Pat Rafter, jubilant after beating Andre Agassi in a thrilling semi-final. A Wimbledon final grudge match, you could say.

The rivalry between Rafter and Sampras can be stemmed back to 1998, when after losing in the final set in Cincinnati, Sampras was asked in a press conference what the difference was between the two players. "Ten Grand Slams" was the reply. An arrogant and dismissive response. "I just got kind of uncharacteristically emotional there, following a tough loss. He took offence and I don't blame him", said Sampras in his book 'Lessons from a Life in Tennis'. Unsurprisingly, "cry baby" was the term Rafter used to describe his compatriot's comments upon hearing them.[5] This only heightened the friction between the pair, adding extra fuel to an already highly publicised Wimbledon final.

Despite the hostile relationship between them, they had several great battles over the years. The duo ended up facing each other over a dozen times on the ATP Tour, with Sampras claiming victory on 12 of their 16 meetings. "Pat was extremely crafty" claims Sampras. "I had a lot of trouble with his serve; it wasn't the pace or the weight of his shots, and it wasn't the speed. It was the way he mixed up his serves, moved them around and kept me guessing. He was an absolute master of picking his service locations".[4]

The final itself was a close, intense battle. Both players started well, and with the score locked at 5-5 in the first set, the British weather decided to play a part. The heavens opened, and staff rushed to drag the covers over centre court as both players evacuated. "The rain delay had special significance for me", said Sampras. "It meant that the cortisone shot would be wearing off earlier in the match than usual". The six time Wimbledon champion felt so close to claiming his seventh title, he was prepared to go against his doctor's advice and have a second injection of the pain reliever, but ultimately chose not to. "The doctor was pretty adamant about not doing that. He said we had touched it enough already. So after the delay I went back out, feeling considerably more uncomfortable than when we had stopped".[4]

He slumped to a 12-10 defeat in the first set tie-breaker. Nervously, and uncharacteristically, double faulting to give Rafter a one set to love lead. If Sampras was going to break Emerson's record, he was going to do it the hard way.

Perhaps the defining moment of the final came in the second set tie-breaker. Rafter raced into a 4-1 lead playing some excellent tennis, and eventually found himself with a couple of set points that would give him a two sets to love cushion. "I thought I was going to lose the match at that point", confessed Sampras. "I guarantee if he'd have won either of those points, he'd have won the title".[4] Unbelievably, perhaps overawed by the occasion, Rafter faltered. The determination, drive, and sheer talent of Sampras had pulled it back. A carefully placed volley sent Rafter the wrong way, clinching the set and bringing the match level. Sampras subsequently won the following set 6-4. A true sign of a champion. He had claimed control of the final at the expense of his right foot. He wasn't completely unable to run on it, but it was getting alarmingly close to that.

Sampras drove on, firing his lightning serve and raced away in the final set. "I was so into the moment that I actually enjoyed the pain. I had a fierce desire to drain every ounce of meaning and every sight, sound and smell out of the moment".[4] In a very one sided fourth set, Sampras stormed to his seventh Wimbledon title, Rafter's return of serve hit the bottom of the net at match point, meaning Sampras once again reigned supreme at the All England Club. 6-7, 7-6, 6-4, 6-2. Remarkable considering the pain he had endured not only in that match, but over the whole tournament. Those two weeks personified who Pete Sampras was. A fighter, somebody who mixed hard work and dedication with amazing natural talent. As former U.S. President Theodore Roosevelt once said, "it is not in the still calm of life that great characters are formed".[6] Champions are made when faced with adversity, and by the time of his seventh Wimbledon win, Sampras had overcome his fair share of hardship.

But how did Sampras get to be the Pete Sampras we all

came to admire? To truly understand how he did this and how he became such a great champion, it's important we go slightly back in time.

A Davis Cup to *Forget*

Before the arrival of Tim Gullikson as his coach in January 1992, Sampras had just come off the back of an extremely disappointing Davis Cup tournament with the United States. The nations watchful eyes twinkled in hope as the spectacular array of star players, including both Pete Sampras and Andre Agassi, took to the court in France.

Sampras' form going into the tournament was that of a roller coaster. He had lost to Brad Gilbert in Sydney, but subsequently won however in Lyon. Back to back losses against Becker in Stockholm then followed a brilliant win at the ATP Finals, considered the fifth most important tournament of the year. Despite being a U.S. Open champion, inconsistency had crept into his game, and he had doubts whether he was the right man to lead his country to an illustrious Davis Cup triumph, where they would face a very good, and extremely motivated French team.

Although being nominated as their lead singles player, Sampras was still considered a "rookie" on the tour. He recalls his nomination as team USA's leading singles player as "like an NFL quarter-back getting his first start in the Super Bowl".[4]

Unsurprisingly perhaps, the tournament got off to the worst possible start for the American. He immediately suffered a sobering loss to Henri Leconte, France's number two player, in front of an electrified French crowd. Leconte was as good as Sampras poor, with winners flying past him regularly.

On the critical final day, a 20-year-old Sampras was pitted against world top ten player and French number one, Guy Forget. Having lost in his first match, team USA needed a Sampras win here to keep their Davis Cup hopes alive. Still trying to heal his wounds from the defeat to Leconte in his previous outing, Sampras struggled both with confidence and with his game, succumbing to Forget in four sets. Sampras was a fragile spirit throughout the match, and when Forget fired an ace right past Sampras to deny him the set, the American's confidence took another brutal hit.

Despite showing signs of why he was nominated as America's number one by winning a set of his own, Sampras couldn't do enough to avoid defeat. Forget saw off a barrage of attacks in the latter half of the match, and in doing so ensured France won their first Davis Cup in 59 years.

Team captain Tom Gorman summed up the failure of the national team by questioning the desire of his players. "The French won all the crucial points at all the important moments over the weekend", scolded Gorman. Sampras was equally as dispirited, as could be seen with him leaving the court disconsolate along with his American teammates. "I felt terrible afterwards. I'd been overwhelmed. One thing was painfully clear by the end of the final against France. Pete Sampras, a raw youth, was completely unprepared for the demands of Davis Cup play", the American himself said years later.[4]

Something needed to change. Everybody could see that he was a fantastic raw tennis player with a brilliant serve and fabulous attacking play; but there was something missing, perhaps a piece of the jigsaw that needed filling. Could this Pete Sampras go on to become a 14-time Grand Slam champion? It's doubtful. Could this 20-year-old have gone on to fight his way to a 7th Wimbledon crown in 2000 with practically one foot? We don't know. But what we know for sure is that after the Davis Cup in 1991, he needed a new coach.

A New Era Begins

"Today, I lost a dear friend and a coach".[7] Those were the words uttered by Pete Sampras after his long-time companion and coach, Tim Gullikson, passed away in May 1996. The success Sampras and Gullikson achieved in their time together is extraordinary. Fitting perhaps, that Sampras used the word "friend" before "coach" when articulating that sentence after Gullikson's untimely passing. Despite their relationship forming in the 90s, Gullikson's impact on Pete Sampras is a key factor in his domination of the men's game throughout the millennium, and why their partnership categorically deserves mentioning in this book.

Almost immediately after the dismay of the Davis Cup in 1991, Sampras employed Tim Gullikson as his full-time coach in January 1992. His previous coach, Joe Brandi, couldn't cope with the relentless travelling that players and coaches must endure on the ATP Tour, and they inevitably parted ways.

At the time, the American was a top ten player in the world, having recently exploded into the spotlight, becoming the youngest player to win the U.S. Open at the age of 19 years and 28 days. A remarkable accomplishment. As previously mentioned however, he often struggled with consistency, a feature so important in every dominant player's game past or present.

"Joe Brandi had been good to have around to crack the whip", Sampras remembered.[4] It is without question Brandi improved Pete's fitness, immediately noticing it as a flaw in his game. "Pete had tremendous potential, but he had never worked on his conditioning. If you're not fit at this level, you won't win anything, let alone a trophy", said Brandi when questioned on his early assessment of Sampras.[8] Brandi certainly had a positive influence on the teenage sensation, as it was under the guidance of the Puerto Rican coach that Sampras first started rising through the world rankings. Evidence of this can be seen in Sampras' standing at the start of the 1990 season. He was just inside the top 100 at number 81 at the start of the year, but became a U.S. Open Champion and top ten player by the end of the following. An impressive couple of years, yet still there seemed to be something missing in the shy and impressionable American's game. "He had worked me hard" said Sampras. "Getting me out early to run, forcing me to take part in two-on-one drills. And while he knew the fundamentals well, I can't think of a single thing he taught me that became part of my secret knowledge as a top pro. It would be very different with Tim".

The U.S. Open win in many ways created problems for the pair. Brandi had never played on the pro tour, he had never experienced what it was like to win a major tournament, and neither had Sampras until that point. "Joe and I both freaked out after I won my first U.S. Open title", he admitted.[4] Sampras now had a reputation to defend, which put immense pressure on them both to live up to the roles the world of tennis had cast them. With Sampras' game not as strong as it may have appeared, doubts over the pair's future began to emerge.[4] Perhaps it was Brandi's lack of experience as a top player himself that led to his inability to propel Sampras to the level he eventually achieved.

It could be that Brandi's style of coaching wasn't flexible enough to take a raw Sampras to the top of world tennis. Nick Bollettieri, founder of the prestigious Nick Bollettieri Tennis Academy, recalls Joe Brandi's coaching methods; "Joe Brandi was a no-nonsense coach who knew only one way to train: hit thousands of balls and get into the best shape of your life".[8] It appeared Brandi had taken Sampras as far as he could.

Sampras had plateaued, his form was inconsistent and his game not at the level it needed to be. When Brandi eventually decided to spend more time with his family at the end of the 1991 season, both men breathed a sigh of relief.[4]

Tim Gullikson was the man chosen to replace Brandi to become Sampras' full-time coach. A significant moment in both men's career, but a turning point that began in relative obscurity.

Although it appears straightforward, the story of how Tim Gullikson ended up coaching Sampras is a rather unique tale. Originally, when looking for a new coach, Sampras reached out to Tom Gullikson, Tim's twin brother. (Yes, their parents really named their twin sons Tim and Tom!) In their playing careers, the siblings had been excellent doubles players. The pair won ten doubles titles together, and brilliantly reached the Wimbledon doubles final in 1983, eventually losing to John McEnroe and Peter Fleming. It was Tim however, the slightly younger of the two (by a few minutes), who was the better player. After reaching a career high of 18th in the world in 1978, Tim went on to reach the quarter-final of SW19 himself the following year, earning an extraordinary straight sets victory over McEnroe in the round of 16.

It was Sampras' agent at the time, Ivan Blumberg, who suggested that Pete met with the Gullikson's. As mentioned above, it was Tom Gullikson, not Tim, who initially met with Sampras with the intention of becoming his coach. After hitting together for a while and discussing the potential partnership, they couldn't come to an agreement. Tom's heavy schedule, which included coaching the brilliant Jennifer Capriati, coincided with his work for Team USA at the Olympics. Such a heavy workload meant he was unable to become Brandi's replacement. Crucially however, Tom had a suggestion. His twin brother and fellow coach, Tim.[4]

After a subsequent meeting, Sampras settled on Tim as the successor to Joe Brandi. Brandi's replacement was a relentless student of the game, and had always planned on becoming a tennis coach.[9] This is surprising, as most former players fall back on coaching once they can no longer compete at the top level. It's a way of remaining in the game and fills the inevitable void that retirement ultimately brings. But this wasn't the case for Sampras' new mentor. Tim was simply born to be a tennis coach. It is said that there comes a time in every leader's life where they feel they have discovered that where they want to be is where they are. Whether that's the leader of a company, an organisation, or a country. It's a voice within them that says "this is the real me, this is my calling".[6] When Tim Gullikson began working with Sampras, he certainly felt that. It wasn't just tennis either, whether he was hitting golf balls with friends or any other sport, Gullikson was always keen to help improve the people around him. An incredibly charming figure who had time for everybody.[9]

*

From the beginning, it was an ideal partnership. His new client represented a dream student for Tim. Sampras was a quiet individual, but always ready to listen to advice. Immensely talented, but still very much raw and open to developing new skills, and this suited Gullikson.[9]

In many ways, they were opposites; Tim, an extrovert, easy going socialite, complemented the more reserved and introverted Sampras. Whilst many people involved in the sport felt distant from one of its star players, everybody adored his new coach. Former world number one Jim Courier perhaps said it best: "Tim was one of the most liked people in my time on the ATP circuit. Everybody loved Gully".[10] This was feasibly the first major difference between Brandi and Gullikson; the relationship they had with their star student off the court. Gullikson and Sampras formed a unique bond immediately. They would often be seeing joking around off court, playing cards or hanging out after training sessions.[4] Conversely, Sampras has often spoken of the difficult relationship he had with Brandi, with the considerable age gap making it an often strenuous alliance.[4]

Life was different with his new coach at the helm, and it wasn't long before things started to improve on the court. At the time, Sampras had never been ranked as the best player in the world, so the objective was clear.

But how did a fantastic doubles player and overachieving singles player provide the impetus to turn a raw Sampras into a record breaking champion?

Implementing Change

It's common for tennis coaches to plan entire practice sessions around a specific shot, with particular emphasis on the mechanics to breed consistency. The aim of this, is to possess an arsenal of shots that can be repeated over and over again, almost embedded in the unconsciousness of a player. Despite having its obvious benefits, structured drills can also be detrimental to a player's game.[11] Aforementioned, Joe Brandi's style was, and still very much is, an accepted method of coaching - using large numbers of repetitions with very little in the way of variation. Sampras would often hit 50 forehands in a row, followed by 50 backhands. As we will see later in this book however, there isn't one singular successful way to coach, with all players needing different methods that suit them specifically. Low variability, or blocked practice, that Sampras used so heavily with his former coach, meant the American's mental effort was considerably low when practicing. This can be described as low contextual interference.[11] On the contrary, the man he appointed to replace Brandi had vastly different ideas when it came to coaching.

When looking at statistical data, research shows that in Grand Slam matches in particular, rallies last between 0-5 shots on average.[12] It therefore makes little sense to spend the majority of a practice session hitting twenty or more ground strokes one after another. Nobody was more aware of this than Tim Gullikson, and he immediately began an overhaul of what

Sampras' training entailed.

One of the first changes Gullikson put into effect was the time Sampras spent out on court on a typical practice day. Although not the first to do it, having borrowed this particular method from Jimmy Connors, it proved effective and is often used by many of the top tennis pros today. Gullikson shortened the length of the training sessions. The duo scrapped long and heavily structured practice that Sampras had become accustomed to under Brandi, playing hours of ground strokes, volleys and serves. Instead, he started to focus on short but intensive practice with refined purpose.[4] This method had worked brilliantly for Connors, the eight time Grand Slam champion, and Gullikson believed it could work for Sampras too. Connors' ideas on training were completely different to many of his competitors throughout the 1970s and 80s, when he won all but the French Open. The majority of players would go out and hit cross-court forehands, cross-court backhands, and so on repeatedly each day, using a blocked style of training. Connors, on the contrary, would limit his sessions to less than an hour.[13] "On the day of a match, I'll go out and practice for about 40 minutes. That's all", he confessed.[13] Amazing really, and judgements were often made about whether a player could keep up with the demands of the game with such little time spent practicing. But it wasn't the quantity of the sessions, it was the quality that counted. Gullikson, with clear inspiration from Connors, found a way to implement first-class practice by picking a weakness and working on it as Sampras played a set or match against a fellow professional. That way, you refrain from using tedious and structured drills.[13] Connors summarised this style of training by saying "in short, set a specific objective for yourself before you walk on the practice court and play a game. There's not much pressure on you to win, and the added challenge is likely to make the game even more exciting. I'm certain you'll also raise the level of your play simply by working towards a goal".[13] This laid the foundation for the Gullikson/Sampras combination. Work hard, play hard.

During Sampras' new training regime, he constantly hit all his best shots, didn't give up on any ball his opponent hit back to him, and kept up an immense work rate throughout.[4] Practicing this way enabled Sampras to steer away from training in a blocked-like system. The randomness in which he was forced to play his shots resulted in greater focus, and a development in his game management.[11] This was the style of coaching that Sampras needed at the time, and massively helped towards his sudden rise in the world rankings.

To coincide with this new, shorter, and less structured way of practicing, Gullikson made technical adjustments to Sampras' game too. At the beginning of their time together, Sampras, although a U.S. Open champion, had gone almost two years without reaching another Grand Slam final. Emerging victorious at Wimbledon had always been a dream for Sampras, and he knew he had to develop his game if he was to realise his ambition. Tim had always excelled on grass, and Wimbledon saw him win arguably his best ever game, that straight sets victory over John McEnroe just over ten years prior. In contrast, Sampras' record at Wimbledon was startlingly poor, losing twice in the first round, and once in the second round during his three attempts. This was an area of expertise for Gullikson, and his wisdom proved pivotal.

Despite his dazzling array of shots, Gullikson, noticing a weakness, immediately started working on Sampras' return of serve, particularly on the backhand side. His inability to return serve effectively on grass was having a detrimental effect on his confidence, perhaps explaining his poor record at the famous All England Club. Gullikson, using his experience of winning plenty of matches on the green surface himself, managed to turn this weakness into a strength.[14] To do this, he shortened Sampras' stroke. From the beginning, Gullikson wasn't impressed with his student's lack of technical discipline, which often led to Sampras using his hands loosely when hitting his shots. Although wrists and hands play a critical role in every shot, you cannot use them to compensate for a lack of work in your arms and body, which generate important power.[4] A player with such incredible touch like Sampras could often get away with this lazy technique, but under Gullikson, he no longer could. This shift in his swing saw Sampras fire far more penetrating shots, with the ball racing to the other side of the court, no longer floating through the air. This in turn made it far more difficult for his opponents to attack, allowing him to take control of matches.[4]

It wasn't just his backhand, either. A staggering amount of technical work went into Sampras' other shots, too. On the backhand volley, Sampras was again suffering from his "handsy" approach when hitting his shots, and this can be seen in many of his pre-Gullikson matches.[4] When volleying, his body was often upright, simultaneously dropping the racquet head low underneath his torso upon impact. This, in turn, left his shot lacking pace and any real penetration to cause his opponent any real concern. The best volleys are hit firm, with the player's body completely behind the racquet to generate power and speed. To achieve this, the duo worked tirelessly on ensuring Sampras got his body further down to the ground to meet the ball, rather than simply lowering his racquet and letting his hands and wrists do the work for him. This meant using his whole body, from his feet, to his legs, and torso. Improving his volley required immense refinement of his positioning, which became a major part of practice for the former U.S. Open champion.[4]

Sampras credits Gullikson for the technical fine-tunings that enabled him to transform his game, with particular emphasis on his grass court playing style. "These tunings all helped, and shortening my backswing on all my returns was of critical importance in my transformation into a good grass-court player", he confessed.[4]

All of the technical work that the pair spent hours working

on went hand in hand with Gullikson's guidance on shot selection. Gone were flashy and inconsistent shots, and in came high percentage tennis. Gullikson somewhat brilliantly compared himself to a basketball coach when speaking of his work with Sampras. "The trick is to teach the guy when he should take the 3-point shot and when he shouldn't" said Gullikson, in his usual charming tone. He then compared Sampras to legendary basketball player Jerry West, known for his arsenal of fantastic long range shots. He wanted his student to be more consistent with his play by cutting out sloppy unforced errors.[7] The new way of training made it far easier than it would have been under Brandi.

Perhaps the most noticeable change that Tim Gullikson brought to Sampras' game was his attitude on court. This was the biggest area of improvement for his coach when identifying flaws.[4] This may sound surprising, as Sampras was known throughout his career as having excellent temperament, often showing little emotion in matches. Rod Laver, the former Australian world number one and 11-time Grand Slam winner, summarised Sampras' level headed persona on court as "phenomenal" in important matches.[15] But in January 1992, that wasn't always the case.

Gullikson noticed something in Sampras that perhaps the casual fan may have not. Or maybe even Sampras himself didn't notice. He would hunch his back on court and droop low, most notably when things weren't going his way.[4] It's very easy to play tennis when you're playing well, I can tell you that from my own experience. Tennis is simple when it seems harder to miss a forehand winner down the line than it does to land it, or when your backhand slice is neutralising your opponent's attacks with devastating effect. You puff your chest out and feel like nothing can stop you. But nobody can play like that all the time. The real challenge, the thing that turns good players into great ones, is the ability to never let your head drop and win matches when you aren't playing your best tennis. Nobody understood this better than Tim.[4] Gullikson himself was somebody who overachieved if you consider his actual ability as a tennis player. What he did superbly however, was use what qualities he did have and maximise them to their fullest potential. This, without doubt, included grinding out results in matches against players who had more natural ability, but never a better attitude or more desire. This is what he planned to instil into a young Pete Sampras, whose game as a competitor was far from fully developed. Tim was determined to drain every ounce of potential from Pete's game from practice sessions, in regards to technical improvements and the mental side too.[4]

The process of turning Sampras into the mentality monster he became wasn't easy. Aforementioned, the two were completely different in terms of people. Getting a player to improve a certain shot or movement on court is one thing, but changing a player's inner mindset is another. Although throughout his career, Sampras was still prone to slouching (he could be forgiven for this due to his sheer size and shape, though), Gullikson instilled in Sampras an inner grit. He removed the softness that had caused inconsistencies in his game, and instead instilled a fighting spirit and never say die attitude.[4] What better example of this than in the 2000 Wimbledon Championships that we spoke about earlier. It would have been so easy for Sampras to cave in, especially during the early rounds, knowing Wimbledon would always come around again next year. But the principles that Sampras had been taught by Gullikson turned him from an inverted prodigy to one of the sport's most celebrated players.

When Richard Neustadt published his timeless study on presidential leadership in 1960, he put forward the argument that temperament is the key factor when separating good leaders from great ones.[16] Gullikson's self-assured, optimistic temperament was no doubt the keystone to his success as a tennis coach. He was able to use his experience of playing himself and adapt seamlessly to his changing circumstances. His attitude was well suited to being a tennis coach, and when a unique opening presented itself to Gullikson in becoming Sampras' new coach, he seized the opportunity. He managed to create a profound, reciprocally dependent bond with his player, as could be seen in full view at the 1995 Australian Open.

*

Doing It For Gully

During the fifth and final set of his quarter-final match with Jim Courier at the 1995 Australian Open, the world saw a side to Pete Sampras that they had never witnessed before. It had been an unimaginably distressing few days for the 24 year old. In front of thousands of fans inside the Rod Laver stadium, Sampras began to cry, uncontrollably. The vulnerability he showed in that moment resonated with the entire crowd, and the millions of people watching on television.

In true Sampras style, he had fought back from two sets to love down and the match was evenly poised at 2 sets all. It was the events before the match however, that had caused the American to break down on court. Gullikson had been diagnosed with a rare cancer and had very little time to live. He had been experiencing health issues for a few months before the diagnosis, but until now, Sampras had, through all his sadness, managed to stay strong and focused on his tennis. Usually when we break down emotionally, we aren't in front of a packed arena, but the same couldn't be said for Pete Sampras that day. "He was so much more than a coach. He was my best friend and someone I've told a lot of things that I've never told anyone", he admitted.[10]

At two sets to one down, he earned himself a set point that, if taken, would see him level the tie. After a powerful forehand right into the corner from Courier, Sampras leaped to his left and just managed to send the ball back. The ball seemed to hang in the air forever, with Courier stood directly underneath, ready to save the set and thrash it past Sampras. In what can only be described as a monumental error, Courier fired his smash miles past the baseline. The Australian crowd burst into life, the roar could be heard from way beyond the stadium. 2-2. Sampras had clawed his way back.

The most memorable part of that match however, was what happened at the start of that fifth and final set. After wiping the tears from his eyes, Sampras regained composure and displayed some of the most fantastic tennis. He hit aces, regularly fired ground stroke winners, and landed beautifully precise volleys past Courier that he had worked on so profusely with Tim. It appeared that everything he had learned from his coach came out all at once in that match. Extremely high level tennis, mixed with mental toughness and tremendous character.

He went on to win that match, and the semi-final that followed, with his best friend and coach at the forefront of his mind. At the end of the Australian Open, where he agonisingly suffered defeat to Andre Agassi in an enthralling final, he dedicated the tournament, and all his future tournaments, to Tim Gullikson.

Together, the pair saw Sampras reach the coveted world number one ranking, a spot that he would go on to claim his own for a record breaking 286 weeks, and four Grand Slam titles. By the time of Gullikson's passing at the age of 44 in 1996, Pete Sampras had risen from a talented but inconsistent teenager, to the best player in the world. He helped Sampras stay competitive when so many of the game's top players were fading into obscurity at the turn of the millennium, amid an upsurge of young powerful baseline players. Although Sampras' success cannot be tied to one single event, person or trait, with Paul Annacone certainly playing a part in his success, the influence of Tim Gullikson on his career will never be forgotten.

The impact Gullikson had, not just on Sampras but on the sport of tennis in its entirety, was recognised in 2019 by the Association of Tennis Professionals (ATP). At the annual ATP awards ceremony, the Tim Gullikson Career Coach Award made its debut, with the aim of showcasing somebody who has inspired generations of players and coaches to help with the growth of the game. The winner must exemplify leadership, excellence, respect, and a true love for the sport. All the attributes that Gullikson himself possessed. Australian Tony Roche was the first recipient of the award, and it's fitting that Tim Gullikson's name will now forever be remembered.

Table 1.1: Pete Sampras Career Grand Slams by Year

1990	1993	1994	1995	1996
U.S. Open	U.S Open Wimbledon	Wimbledon Australian Open	U.S. Open Wimbledon	U.S. Open

1997	1998	1999	2000	2002
Wimbledon Australian Open	Wimbledon	Wimbledon	Wimbledon	U.S Open

Chapter Two

2

Shaping Roger Federer

*"Roger can produce tennis shots that should be
declared illegal".*

Tracy Austin

IDENTIFYING KEY HISTORICAL MOMENTS is an easy task in
hindsight, but even at the time, Roger Federer's Wimbledon
victory over Pete Sampras in July 2001 felt like a landmark day
in tennis. Sampras himself defined the moment as being the
day he "passed the Wimbledon baton" over to Roger Federer.[4]

Up until that moment, The All England Club belonged
to the American. As the seven time champion walked onto
court that day to face a 19-year-old Roger Federer, nobody
realistically envisaged anything but victory for Sampras. He

raced to the fourth round, having beaten Francisco Clavet, Britain's Barry Cowan, and Sargis Sargsian along the way, dropping a mere two sets in the process. Despite not being in his usual scintillating form throughout the 2001 season, he was on the hunt for his fifth consecutive Wimbledon title, and it was going to take an almighty effort to stop him.

The man on the opposite side of the court was the teenage former Wimbledon junior champion, Roger Federer. It was a dream draw for the young Swiss sensation, making his centre court debut. Behind Boris Becker and Sweden's Stefan Edberg, Federer positioned Sampras as his third favourite player growing up.[17] As he walked out onto centre court on that summer's afternoon, with Sampras following just behind, he exuded confidence. His shoulders wide and his chest puffed out. He looked a player who had been a regular on tennis' Sistine Chapel for years. It was a court that had seen many of his idols make their name, and Federer saw no reason why today couldn't be his day to launch himself into the spotlight. "I'm not going to play to win a set or just to look good" he declared beforehand, "I am going to play to win".[17] Although they may seem like outlandish comments, considering Sampras' record on grass and wealth of experience, they weren't crazy. Federer had actually played a better season than his opponent so far that year. The youngster had won his maiden ATP Tour tournament in Milan just months earlier, defeating Julien Boutter in straight sets in the final, as well as beating multiple top ten players throughout the course of the 2001 season. He appeared to relish playing higher ranked players, where he often played his best tennis. Despite this, Wimbledon's American king was still the comfortable favourite. Everything was set for a true Wimbledon showdown.

The opening set was a close, tight affair. Both players served impeccably, with Federer attacking aggressively, often rushing to the net in a style that we rarely saw from him in later years. Neither man could find the all important breakthrough however, and the first set ended with a tie-break. Here, it was Sampras who gained the advantage and saw himself earn the first set-point. Federer, who had been labelled somewhat hot-headed and prone to a lack of concentration, needed to dig deep and show what he was made of. On the verge of losing the set, he tossed the ball in the air, bent his knees, and fired a thunderous ace past the Sampras. Almost in the blink of an eye, he'd completely turned it around against the Wimbledon champion. He roared in ecstasy before walking back to his seat. He'd won the tie-break and was now 1-0 up, showing immense character in the process.

In a back and forth second set, the pair continued to battle, showing tennis of the highest calibre. "Very early in the match I realised I was up against a kid with a complete game and talent to burn", confessed Sampras. "He was poised and dignified, but he played with great flair".[4] Federer was playing tennis way beyond his years, showing glimpses of the player he would go on to become. The feeling inside centre court that day began to shift. This relatively unknown teenager had not only come to play, he had come to win. It was Sampras however, showing the grit and determination that we saw in the previous chapter, who found a breakthrough in the second set, breaking serve and clinching it 7-5. You could be forgiven for thinking it was 'business as usual' when Sampras levelled the tie, but Roger had other ideas. The tennis he displayed in the third set was flawless, and he deservedly went 2-1 up. After regrouping and heading back out for the fourth set, it was Sampras this time who upped his game. He took his serving up a notch and played some hugely effective volleys. After winning set-point, the centre court crowd rose to their feet. The tie was heading towards a Hollywood style finish.

With the score locked and both men on four games each in the fifth and final set, Federer faced his biggest test of the match, and perhaps his career so far. At 30-30, the youngster fired a serve to Sampras' body. He rushed to the net, looking to win the point with a serve and volley tactic that had worked so well all tournament. Sampras, showing the coolness that had earned him all those Grand Slam titles, effortlessly shifted his feet, pulled back his racquet, and eloquently hit a trademark one-handed backhand. It fizzed through the air, over the net, and straight past the outstretched Federer. An outrageously brilliant shot. 30-40. Sampras had break point, meaning if taken, he'd be serving for the match. Federer had work to do. This time, he served to the right of Sampras, to his forehand, and immediately set off towards the net again. After a brilliantly cushioned forehand half-volley off the return, Federer followed it up with a venomous backhand volley, wrong footing Sampras, leaving him with no chance to return. He'd levelled the score. After a game that seemed to last an age, around 5 minutes in total, it was Federer who came out on top, putting himself 5-4 up. A dazzling display of determination. This proved to be his defining moment. Sampras' dominance of this tournament was suddenly in serious danger of coming to an abrupt end. Rather than serving to win the match, he was now serving to stay in the tournament. This was no ordinary player on the other end of the court and by now, everybody watching had realised.

It was of course Roger who went on to win that final set, falling to his knees after smashing a return winner past Sampras at match point, letting out every emotion that had built up over the previous few hours. Tennis had just given birth to its newest, and soon to be, most dominant star. That match symbolised the end of an era. Sampras' 31 match unbeaten run at Wimbledon had ended, and who better to do it than the man who would become synonymous with centre court for many years to come. It was the biggest win of Federer's career, and the start of a remarkable journey that would see him, at the time of writing this, lift twenty Grand Slam titles. But who are the coaches behind this unprecedented success? It would be unfair to mention just one. To get a firm understanding, let's go back to the very start of his rise to greatness.

*

The Old Boys Tennis Club

When a young Roger Federer turned up at The Old Boys Tennis Club in his hometown of Basel, Switzerland, he immediately caught the eye of its head tennis pro, Adolf Kacovsky. "I noticed right away that this guy was a natural talent", boasted Kacovsky. "He was born with a racquet in his hand".[17] To begin with, Roger just took part in group sessions with the other players his age, but soon added individual lessons to his practice, where Kacovsky, keen to get to work with Federer, could give him special attention. It soon became apparent that the young boy from Basel was an extremely quick learner. He could learn more swiftly, and understand more deeply compared to other boys his age. With his parents happy to finance his lessons, the beginning of Federer's rise to greatness can be stemmed back to this time.[18] To coincide with his natural ability and ferocious pace in which he picked up new skills, he was highly ambitious. He would often tell people of how he wanted to become the best player in the world, much to the amusement of his friends and even his coach. "I thought he would perhaps become the best player in Switzerland or Europe, but not the best in the world", confessed Kacovsky.

One of Rogers biggest rivals in his very early days of playing tournaments was a fellow Swiss youngster who was six months his elder, Danny Schnyder. He too could see talent in Federer, but not enough to take him all the way to the pinnacle of the sport. "I was surprised to see Roger suddenly storm to the top.

One noticed that he had good strokes at 11 or 12, but I never would have thought that he would become the number one player in the world" he recalled.[17]

Perhaps the most flawed habits of Federer's early years on court was his lack of seriousness when practicing, and this could be an argument as to why he wasn't seen as a future legend of the game to begin with. "My parents always said 'start training better', but I often had problems getting motivated", admitted Roger. He'd often lose to a player in practice, but win comfortably against the same opponent in a tournament.[17] After winning his first national tennis tournament aged 11, he had a decision to make. Before he had even become a teenager, Roger had to decide which sport he wanted to put his heart and soul into. This was absolutely a turning point for the young Swiss hopeful. Like many top athletes, he tried his hand at a number of sports when he was young. None more so perhaps than football. After impressively becoming the national under 12 champion, the task of deciding which sport he should dedicate himself to became progressively more important. "My soccer coach eventually told me that if I didn't attend all the sessions he couldn't really put me in the team for matches at the weekend", said Federer. "I couldn't make all the matches anyway because I was also trying to play tennis tournaments. I knew that I couldn't do both soccer and tennis until I die, so I eventually made the decision to go for tennis".[17] With his parents both keen tennis players, the decision to choose tennis over football shouldn't really come as a shock, and it's a decision that Federer unsurprisingly doesn't look back on with regret!

Despite his victory at the national tournament and gradual increase in ability, he needed something, or somebody, that could take all his natural talent and mould it into something special. There are countless stories of Federer breaking down during matches when he was younger, smashing racquets to bits or failing to fight back tears after a loss. What he needed was further guidance to coincide with the coaching with Kacovsky, both on and off the court, and in Peter Carter, he found that.

Peter Carter

When Peter Carter accepted an offer from the The Old Boys Tennis Club in 1993, he was tasked with building a mentoring programme for the younger players. In and amongst all the youth players associated with the club at the time, there was Roger Federer.

Carter, a blonde haired and blue eyed Australian, was a compassionate and friendly individual. Although a decent player in his prime, his career was hampered by a series of injuries that stopped him from reaching his true potential. A career high of 173 is an indication of that. Nevertheless, the 25-year-old got to work in his new environment in Basel and immediately had a profound impact on Federer.[18] Having been coached by Adolf Kacovsky since joining the club, it was the Australian coach who was now beginning to have the biggest impact on the 12-year-old since his arrival. It wasn't just Federer either, every player at the club reaped the benefits of Carter's employment. Madeleine Bärlocher, the lady responsible for hiring Carter, was impressed with the way he brought the best out of the players. "The training with Peter was perfect, both in tennis terms and on a human level" recalled Bärlocher. "Peter was very personable but very restrained. If a youngster had problems, he'd always take them aside and talk with them. He could talk very well with the juniors". It appeared this was just what Federer needed. Somebody to act as as mentor as much as a pure tennis coach.

The most stark contrast from any other person around him at the time, was that in Peter Carter, Roger had a man who agreed with him when he said he was going to be the best player in the world. He felt in his heart that Federer could go on to do amazing things in the game of tennis. It wasn't usual for Peter to talk like that. He'd ring his friends and tell them of this star player he had on his hands. The confidence he had in Roger breathed life into the youngster. It wasn't long before he became more than a tennis coach, he became a big brother.[17]

Aforementioned, despite excelling in tournaments, Federer often lacked the desire to train before Carter arrived. Marco Chiudinelli, an old friend of Federer's who used to practice with him at the Old Boys Club recalls their training sessions: "It was pretty loud when we were in training" he said. "We talked more than we trained. Training didn't seem too important to us. We just wanted to have a good time and we goofed around a lot".[17] This assessment perfectly summed up the attitude Federer had towards training. He liked to have fun, working hard during sessions wasn't his main focus. That was an area that the Australian coach looked to develop. Carter seemed to have an admirable ability to tell each player exactly what they needed to improve. The general consensus around the club was that whilst Kacovsky was a brilliant teacher, considerably improving the technical side of Federer's game, it was Carter who had the ability to take him to the next level.[18] Whilst offering an arm around the shoulder if a player needed it, Carter could also, on the contrary, be a stern and serious figure when he felt he had to be. If somebody behaved badly on court, as Federer and his friends were often prone to, he didn't stand for it. Seeing Roger sent home early from practice, or sending him out on a long distance run as punishment for poor behaviour, was not a rare occurrence.[18] It may sound harsh, considering his age, but it was this new firmness that saw Federer begin to get the most out of his training sessions. Previous to this, there was a common opinion amongst those at the club that Roger may squander his talent amid concerns his constant joking around and overall lack of discipline would halt his progress.[18]

Federer's desire to train needed work, and it was going to

take somebody special to overcome this downfall. Motivation can vary on a number of different factors when it comes to tennis, and it's no secret that a player's coach plays a pivotal role in their drive, performance and competition efficiency.[19] Research conducted by Kajtna et al. at the University of Ljubljana, found that the main characteristics of all top coaches include persistence, innovation, leadership capabilities, and compatibility. These qualities go a long way in increasing a player's motivation in all aspects of the game, including a hunger to train.[20] Under Carter's tutelage, Roger experienced a coach who put all his focus into him. Whilst coming down hard on Roger at certain times, he was always keen to praise, give guidance at every opportunity, and was always on hand to support his player both on and off the court. This, in turn, helped a young Roger Federer experience more enjoyment out of the sport, subsequently resulting in more effort when practicing and competing.[20] Carter deserves immense praise for helping to switch Federer's mentality.

To coincide with the issues surrounding Federer's commitment to training, he also struggled greatly with his on court outbursts. If you watched Roger Federer play in a tennis match today, you would find a calm and composed figure completely in control of his emotions. If you switched on the television and looked at Roger in the middle of a set, it would be difficult to know if he was winning or losing without looking at the score. He personifies the definition of keeping a cool head, a trait that has seen him earn plaudits around the world. But back at The Old Boys Tennis Club in the early 1990s, it couldn't have been more different. "When things weren't going the way he wanted, he would curse and toss his racquet", said Kacovsky. "It was so bad, I had to intervene sometimes". Federer himself claimed that his attitude on court wasn't good enough when he assessed the situation years later. He confessed to regularly throwing his racquet to the ground and swearing, much to the dismay of his parents. His mother at one point threatened to stop attending Federer's matches if he continued to show such an appalling temperament. His father agreed.[17] Carter, displaying the calm and personable demeanour he was known for, managed to instill principles and values in Roger over the ten years they worked together. A difficult task, and credit must go to his coach for this monumental change in the mindset of his player.

Whilst Peter Carter was consistent in his views on Federer's generational talent on court, he placed even greater emphasis on the youngster's character. He taught the young prodigy how to respect those around him. How to control himself in situations both on and off the court. Carter wanted to see Federer grow into a decent human being, and use tennis as a medium.[21] These values that were instilled in Federer paid dividends over the course of his career, particularly in difficult patches when he wasn't winning as regularly as he once had. No matter what the situation, he was able to remain calm and get back to playing his most brilliant tennis, and still does to this day. Whilst flashes of anger and sobbing still appeared in Rogers game infrequently during those early years at the club, the perfect combination of Adolf Kacovsky and Peter Carter was starting to pay off. Federer's game slowly started to reach new levels. Whilst the former did most of the hands on work, fine tuning all Federer's shots on the court, Carter refined the elements of his game and was a major influence off it. Carter in particular is credited as the man who took all the elements of Roger's game and put them together.[18] The impact on Federer as a person developed significantly thanks to his young Australian coach, but he should also be given credit for his on court coaching ability.

Despite initially being taught his ground strokes and all round game by Kacovsky, the first glimpses of Federer's trademark classical one-handed backhand can actually be traced back to Carter, who himself used a very similar technique in his playing days. Although not the strongest of shots to begin with, the framework was put in place in Basel for Roger to eventually master the art of the one-handed backhand. A shot that would earn him fans, win him countless important points, and impress millions around the world. People loved the way Peter played, and as the saying goes, you teach what you know. The resemblance in Roger and Peter's game is uncanny.[21]

In regards to Kacovsky, it's unfortunate that he didn't get the send off he deserved at The Old Boys Tennis Club. He was the first coach to ever give Roger individual sessions. He, along with Carter, was a huge fan of the one-handed backhand, and it was through his advice that Roger actually chose to use just a singular hand for that particular shot. Just before Kacovsky's 65th birthday in 2006, he was told by The Old Boys Club that his services were no longer needed, with insurance reasons at the forefront of the decision. It was a quiet and subtle send off for Kacovsky, who had coached at the club for almost 40 years.[18]

Ecublens

By the time Roger Federer had turned 14, it was time to put the relentless work the coaching duo of Kacovsky and Carter had done to the test. His game had been gradually developed in Basel, where an immense amount of focus was put into his technical skills, footwork and fully body coordination. The National Tennis Centre in Ecublens, Switzerland, however, was the natural progression for Federer, who had outgrown his hometown tennis club. Here was a good opportunity to play against better players, and the facilities at the National Tennis Centre were a far-cry from his little hometown club. His new home allowed him to add to his game, with additional emphasis on the physical side of the sport.[11] It would give the teenager the chance to focus on his tennis full-time, too, so it made perfect sense on paper. The one downside to this, however, was that joining The National Tennis Centre meant leaving the tutelage of Peter Carter, his coach, and by that time, good friend. Federer struggled in his first few months in his new environment, and there were a number of times he packed his things demanding to go home. He always ended up unpacking however, and stayed on at the facility for many years.

In 1997, the National Tennis Centre expanded and much to the delight of Federer, Peter Carter was brought in as part of the coaching staff. Annemarie Rüege, who at the time was in charge of social integration, was keen to get Carter working with Roger again. "He was brought in under the ulterior motive that he could be paired with Roger", she explained. It was simple really, Federer trained better when Carter was around. He excelled under his guidance at a rate he didn't under other coaches. Carter was therefore brought in to provide special individual coaching to the teenager.[17]

Federer impressed during his time in Ecublens, and everybody was keen for him to reach his potential. Peter Lundgren, a coach at the centre at the time, also began working with Roger, to coincide with his sessions with Carter. Federer became completely engrossed in his tennis towards the mid to late 90s whilst training at Ecublens and subsequently "The House of Tennis" in Biel. "The House of Tennis" was the name given to the new National Tennis Centre in Switzerland and was an upgrade on the facilities in Ecublens. It had multiple courts with a variety of surfaces, enabling the young stars to prepare themselves efficiently for eventually turning professional. Roger knew he had an immense talent, and the work Carter did with him to ensure he focused intently on his training was a huge help towards that. Roger's parents, impressed with the work Carter had done, further stressed the importance of working hard to their son. "We wanted to see results", confessed Lynette Federer. "We made it very clear to Roger that we could not financially support him for ten years so that he could dangle around 400 in the world rankings". It was in 1998, at the age of 16, that he took the giant leap forward and made the decision to become a professional tennis player, after completing his mandatory 9 years in school.[17]

Federer set off on the ATP Tour and immediately started to make an impression. By the year 2000, he was amongst the top junior tennis players in the world, winning the Wimbledon junior tournament along the way, eventually finding himself inside the top 50 in the world rankings. The early work by Adolf Kacovsky and the wisdom provided by Carter had proved to be worth its weight in gold. Federer now had his sights set on reaching the top 25, and there were no doubts he could achieve his goal. It therefore wasn't a surprise that when Federer made a decision in 2000 to change his coach, it raised more than a few eyebrows.

*

Peter Lundgren

Little by little, Peter Carter had started to share the role as Federer's tennis coach with Peter Lundgren at the National Tennis Centre. It had benefited Federer, and the arrangement worked well. Lundgren had played the game at a higher level than the Australian, earning a career high of number 25 in the world at his peak. The experience that he gained from playing at such an elite level provided Federer with knowledge that he couldn't necessarily gain with Carter, whose career was over by the time he was in his mid 20s.[22] All in all however, the duo did provide another perfect combination for the newly turned pro, following the previous combination of Carter and Kacovsky.

With his career thriving but still very much in its infant stage, the Swiss junior Wimbledon champion decided he needed somebody to travel with him on the tour full-time.[18] As we have seen previously, being a pro on the ATP Tour is demanding. The schedule is tough, whether you're a player or a coach. Being on the tour means spending months away from home, distant from family and friends and the home comforts you become accustomed to. With tournaments played around the world throughout the year, the constant travelling coincides with countless nights spent in hotels, and it can easily catch up on you. As a player, deciding who to bring with you is of critical importance in regards to coaching. Not only will the person chosen be your tennis coach, they'll be your best friend whilst you're out there, often spending hours killing time together in between practice sessions and matches. Around the turn of the millennium, Roger had that decision to make. Both men were keen to continue working with their pupil, but ultimately Roger knew he could only choose one of them.

"It was a decision where everybody was sure he was going to take Carter", remembers Yves Illegro, a childhood friend of Roger. After all, the bond Carter and Roger had built up over the ten years they had worked together was undoubtedly stronger than the bond he had with Lundgren, his coach of just three years at the time.[18] Still, it was a difficult decision for Roger, and one he made off the premises of his gut feelings. "It was a toss-up", he recalled. When he listened to his gut feeling however, he felt it was telling him to pick Lundgren. The decision therefore was made, and Peter Carter was no longer the coach of Roger Federer. This came as a surprise to the people around him, and to the tennis world too, who by now were aware of the influence Carter had made on Federer. Whilst extremely disappointed, Carter departed amicably, and bared no resentment to Roger for his decision. Darren Cahill, a close friend of Carter and former coach to Lleyton Hewitt, claimed the coach from Adelaide was very upset, despite outwardly showing a lack of emotion. Carter truly believed he could take Roger to the top of the tennis world. He'd proved countless times over the past decade that he was influential to Roger in regards to the emotional side of tennis, helping him deal with problems both on and off the court. Despite all this, Federer, whilst eternally grateful to Carter, wanted to head in a new direction. "Maybe Roger was looking at it that Carter had got him to a certain level and he needed someone of Lundgren's experience to take him to the next level", said Cahill.[18] Nevertheless, as soon as the decision was made, Lundgren had full control over the Swiss player. To the surprise of some, it would soon become clear that Federer had actually chosen a coach who was incredibly compatible with him.[17]

If you look at Peter Lundgren, he doesn't look like your typical tennis coach. Throughout his playing days on the tour, he could often be seen strutting his guitar and listening to his favourite type of music, hard rock. By the time he retired from playing and began to focus on coaching, his long hair, goatee beard, and large body type didn't give off the impression that the Swede was involved in high level sport. His playing career however was fruitful, and completely outshone the achievements of Roger's former coach, Peter Carter. Lundgren had played on all the famous courts, he'd played against and sometimes beaten a lot of Federer's current opponents, and had earned over a million pounds in prize money. He was a well-known and valued individual on the ATP Tour.[17]

There were areas of Lundgren's game that were eerily alike to Federer's, too. He was prone to smashing a racquet, using foul language and lacking a professional on court persona.

The pair had a distinctly similar character. Lundgren was a naturally easy-going, positive man who was quick witted and funny, and the same can be said about Roger. Whilst it's virtually impossible to pinpoint exactly what should be expected from a coach, it's true that every player requires something different. There isn't really a one-fits-all approach to tennis coaching. Only players themselves know for sure if what their coach is offering is what they need at that time. In Lundgren, Federer clearly felt that he was in the best hands at that stage of his career. In a way that resembled Peter Carter, Lundgren similarly had strong beliefs that Federer was a phenomenal talent that could without doubt go on to become the best player in the world. "I was No. 25 in the world but a long way away from his level. This guy is something special. He's from another planet", uttered Lundgren when he first took over from Carter as his main coach.[17] There was still work to do to elevate Federer to the top of the rankings however.

Winning Ugly

Unsurprisingly, due to Lundgren's love of guitar and music, he first compared Federer to that of a musician. "He is an artist", he said. "When his strokes don't work, he becomes irritated and loses his concentration", comparing Federer's strokes to strings on a musician's instrument. The partnership didn't get off to the best start if you base it off immediate on court results. He lost in the first round at Wimbledon to Yevgeny Kafelnikov of Russia, as well as other countless first round defeats across the tour. In his first 38 ATP Tour tournaments, Federer was beaten in the first round in 21 of them. There were clear flaws in his game, and it was obvious that Lundgren had his work cut out. Despite being a top junior player, having won the Wimbledon Junior Championships in 1998, Federer's prior achievements didn't necessarily mean he would go on to become a leading player in the adult game. For example, South Africa's Wesley Whitehouse won the junior Wimbledon tournament in 1997, a year before Roger, and achieved a career high of only 214 in the ATP rankings. Jurgen Melzer, the Austrian who won the tournament a year after Federer, failed to get past the fourth round of a Grand Slam until he was eliminated in the semi-final of the French Open in 2010. Federer's poor start to life on the ATP Tour was certainly not an anomaly, as success at junior level does not always translate to success on the pro tour. Underneath all the poor results however, positive work was taking place on the practice court.[17]

"Roger has to be able to win in an ugly way", confessed Lundgren amidst all of the frustrating first round losses. "He can do anything with the ball, but he has to learn how to simplify his game". Despite having an arsenal of impressive strokes, Federer was too focused on playing perfectly rather than playing in a way that resulted in victories; as Winston Churchill said, "perfection can also be spelled paralysis". Beautiful topspin forehands don't mean anything if you're afraid to use that other shot that isn't so brilliant.

The most noticeable flaw in Federer's game at this stage was his apparent refusal to come to the net and volley. When he'd play matches, you could often count on one hand the amount of volleys Federer actually played. He simply hated them, and therefore didn't use them, according to Lundgren. His Swiss player had to learn that simply playing shots he had mastered would only get him so far.[17] Lundgren also confessed that whilst he didn't need to do much work with Federer's forehand, with just tactical improvements needed, it was his backhand, serve and volley that needed the most work.[21]

Firstly, the duo worked on Roger's ability to cover the net. At the time, Federer didn't quite know how to do it, which led to him staying at the baseline for the vast majority of his shots. Federer's first round Wimbledon loss to Kafelnikov mentioned earlier was a prime example of that. Kafelnikov, a former world number one and excellent baseline player, hit a young Roger off the court. Winner after winner would fly past him, much to the Swiss' frustration. Although Lundgren already knew this, it was the match against the Russian at Wimbledon that forced Roger to realise it, too. He had to improve his net game.

Lundgren worked tirelessly with him, not just working on the shot itself and its execution, but on his positioning. The theory was that no matter how bad a player's return is on grass, it's always hard to get back, with the ball bouncing so low. If you serve and volley however, it forces the opponent to hit a good return, as a poor one will leave a good opportunity for the server to volley it home. As Lundgren confessed, it took Roger a while to come to grips with charging to the net after serving as he was so used to playing from the baseline. It took time, but Federer slowly started implementing this tactic into his game with the guidance of Lundgren.

In the space of a few short years, the volley became one of Federer's most used shots. At the Australian Open in 2005, a year Roger stormed to victory, he went to the net 85 times throughout the tournament, and when doing so, won around 80 per-cent of the points. A remarkable return, and a stat that shows the ability his coach had in guiding Roger, giving him the confidence to add the shot to his game.

In regards to Federer's serve, Lundgren again worked wonders. If you look back at his serve from the early 2000s, and compare that to the same shot in the mid 2000s, the change is subtle, but crucial. "We made progress with the mechanics of his serve" said Lundgren.[21] His ball toss was often too low, which in turn meant he couldn't bend his knees down far enough to generate more speed. He was asked by Lundgren to change this, tossing the ball up slightly higher before firing. This slight tweak at the start of his serve meant Federer could get lower to the ground and propel himself higher, generating more power and speed in the process. The duo managed to achieve this improvement without affecting Federer's magnificent ability to barely change the motion of his serve no matter where he positioned it.

The most important area of Federer's game that Lundgren was able to develop was the tactical side. The Swede's tactical acumen was fantastic. He was able to use all his experience of playing on the tour to effectively construct game plans for each opponent whilst successfully spotting weaknesses in a player's game for Federer to exploit.[18] The pair would often train for specific opponents, working on areas that would target their flaws. Federer still uses some of these game plans and tactics today. For example, the short and deep tactic. There was a practice drill that the duo used throughout their seven years together that helped to implement this tactic during matches. The drill involved a short back-hand slice to bring an opponent forward, followed by a deep shot to the back of the court to send the opponent to the baseline, leaving them scrambling to get back in time to return. Federer would then shoot forward, ready to pounce on his opponent's weak and usually defensive shot. This meant he could either hit an easy running forehand or volley to win the point. Although most often used against players who didn't want to come to the net because of their lack of volleying skills, it was used against most other opponents too. "Roger used this pattern against almost every player" confessed Lundgren when doing a TV interview years after their split. "Some people just play from the baseline, back to back, but I think it's important to use the whole court". This is a far-cry from the early style of play that Federer used. Rather than playing all his shots from the baseline like he used to (as good as they were), he had now added another dimension to his game, involving playing shots from all areas of the court to devastating effect. Lundgren deserves immense credit for the way he improved Roger's game, both tactically and technically.

Lundgren has never hidden from the fact he made a lot of mistakes throughout his playing career, and he was keen to make sure those same mistakes didn't happen to his pupil. Federer, speaking in 2001, said this: "We get along very well. He's played on the tour and he made a lot of errors when he was a player. He doesn't want me to do the same. He gives me a lot of good advice regarding the other players' weaknesses and strengths and it's going really well". Similar to Federer's old coach, Peter Carter, he was also aware that tennis coaching is as much to do with what is said off the court, as on it. He had a knack of choosing his words carefully. Lundgren knew when to talk, and when not to talk, perhaps learning from experiences he had gained from his own coaches years earlier. Sometimes after a match, Lundgren wouldn't say anything to Roger about what had happened. Other times, he'd spend a great deal of time going through the match and dissecting the performance. It's true that silence is the respite of the confident and the strong, and Lundgren knew when to pick his moments - a crucial trait for any tennis coach. Naturally, it wasn't long before Federer and his coach began to achieve success, and on a summer's day in 2003, it all sensationally clicked together.

A New King Is Born

Roger Federer's first Grand Slam triumph came at a time when the tennis world were starting to question if he would ever reach the top of the game. From 1999-2003, despite excelling under Lundgren, he was still prone to a lack of concentration. He had achieved some excellent results, including that famous win over Sampras at Wimbledon a couple of years earlier, but seemed to lack the killer instinct in big moments. Whenever Roger played in the Davis Cup for his country however, it was different. Here he had extra motivation to concentrate as he had the eyes of Switzerland watching him hit every stroke. He had more responsibility.[18]

With seven time champion Pete Sampras announcing his retirement from the sport a few weeks before the start of Wimbledon in 2003, and last year's Australian champion, Lleyton Hewitt, going through a patchy spell of form, Federer had his best chance of making an impact on the tournament. Everything he had worked on with Lundgren over the previous few years had been leading up to this point. It was here that Federer could turn himself from a perennial prodigy to genuine world class player, and a major contender for the sport's most coveted prizes. He had improved his game technically, and could now play shots from all over the court. He still possessed fantastic baseline shots, but crucially he was now capable of changing things up and using the net if he had to. His serve had improved, and so had his footwork. This had been a problem for him in past Wimbledon tournaments, but not anymore.

Lundgren would often use a specific drill with Roger to improve his footwork. He would feed three balls. Federer had to hit an inside out forehand, a running forehand, and then a short forehand from the middle of the court. Hitting those three shots in succession means moving your feet an awful lot, subsequently improving your footwork. Despite the rest of the world not believing it, Federer and Lundgren felt ready to take the next step at a major tournament to coincide with his performances at the Davis Cup. On Lundgren's advice, Federer, rather than renting a big fancy house in the capital throughout his stay during Wimbledon, rented a small and simple apartment. He isolated there, away from everybody, apart from his girlfriend Mirka, his physiotherapist, and of course his coach, Peter Lundgren himself. He was focused like never before.[17]

Although it may surprise you, Federer's most impressive game at Wimbledon that year wasn't the final. It was his semi-final match against American Andy Roddick that made people stand up and realise he was a serious candidate to become the new champion. Lundgren himself confessed to never having seen Roger play a better match.[17]

There was one singular point during that Federer semi-final masterclass that left a lasting impression on those watching. At 5-3 up in the second set and with set-point, Federer showed perfectly how far Lundgren had taken him. With both men at the back of the court rallying from the baseline, smashing forehands and backhands for what seemed like an age, Federer hit a thunderous forehand cross-court. He then immediately followed it up with a bullet forehand down the line to Roddick's backhand. Federer, doing something he would never have dreamed of just a couple years prior, darted to the net. Roddick's weak backhand shot landed well inside the service box, leaving Federer to hit an outrageously skilled forehand half-volley in the opposite corner. It's a shot that involved everything. Footwork, incredible touch, perfect technique, and confidence. A remarkable shot worthy of winning any Wimbledon semi-final set. "That is impossible!" shouted John McEnroe, who was on the commentary team for America's NBC. Federer himself couldn't help but crack a smile, and beamed all the way back to his seat having just cruised to a two sets to love lead. Lundgren, who was sat in the players' box, jumped to his feet. The pair were on the their way to a Grand Slam final. The third set was straightforward. 7-6, 6-3, 6-3, a dominant performance against a very good player in Andy Roddick.

In the final, Federer did play an Australian, but it wasn't the Australian people had expected. The reigning champion Lleyton

Hewitt was eliminated in the first round and instead, Roger was pitted against the big serving Mark Philippoussis. Despite the Aussie having more experience in similar matches, having previously taken part in the 1998 U.S. Open final, his game wasn't as complete as Roger's, and more importantly, he didn't have Peter Lundgren in his players' box.

Despite Philippoussis having a reputation as a big server, on the day of the final, he was out served and out aced by Federer. The Swiss player out-aced his opponent by 21 to 14. The adjustments Lundgren had made to his serve as well as the religious practicing had certainly paid off.

It was tactically, however, where Federer was most impressive in the final. As we have seen, Lundgren's ability to construct game plans and strategies to counter opponents' strengths set him apart from other coaches. He gave Federer the blueprint on how to beat Philippoussis. Lundgren knew it would be a completely different match than that of his previous one against Roddick. He raised awareness of the Australian's tendency to serve and volley. To counter this, he told Federer to stand closer to the baseline when returning, and refrain from simply blocking it back as he had done against Roddick. As we talked about earlier, serve and volleying on grass requires a better return of serve, so Lundgren knew standing closer to the baseline and hitting a good return was paramount. Hitting his returns closer to the ground, closer to Philippoussis' feet, was one of his main pieces of advice.[17]

Federer followed the game plan perfectly. In a straight forward match and a final he dominated from start to finish, he raced to a straight sets victory. 7-6, 6-2, 7-6. He'd won Wimbledon, dropping just one set to Mardy Fish in the third round on his way. After seeing Philippoussis' shot hit the net on match point, Federer fell to his knees as the Chair Umpire said those three famous words, "Game, Set, Match". As he rose to his feet, he threw his arms in the air, and immediately looked over at Peter Lundgren in the players' box, along with his partner Mirka. His coach had helped him turn his potential into greatness. At the tender age of 21, Roger was a Wimbledon champion and at the start of his Grand Slam journey that would see him rewrite the record books.

If you look back to a few years earlier, when Federer was heading out in the first round of so many tournaments, the words of Lundgren proved to be true. The Swede said over and over again, that once Federer started to win major trophies, he simply wouldn't stop.[23] How right he was. Throughout their working relationship, the duo won 11 titles together, with the highlight of course being his first Wimbledon title and Grand Slam win in 2003.

At the end of the 2003 season, Federer and Lundgren parted ways. The Swedish coach had overseen the most successful period in Roger's career and had helped to completely transform his game. Federer however, just like he was years prior when he split from Carter, was keen to head in a new direction in regards to his coaching. "I just had the feeling I should look for something new. I would like new impetus, and after thinking it over carefully, I saw this as a solution for next year", said Federer at the time. The two men, both with similar haircuts and characters, were seen as inseparable, and the decision was again met with scepticism.[24]

The theme of regularly changing coaches runs throughout Roger's career. He often conducts interviews and hires and fires his coaches in a way similar to a CEO dealing with consultants.[25] When the 20-time Grand Slam champion posted an Instagram post in 2018, paying homage to all the coaches who had been a part of his journey, the list was rather large. Peter Lundgren, Peter Carter, José Higueras, Stefan Edberg, Paul Annacone, Severin Luthi, Ivan Ljubicic, and Adolf Kacovsky were all present on the list. All of these men had an impact on the career of Federer, all offering him what he needed at the time. The impact of Peter Lundgren and Peter Carter as we have seen however, propelled him onto the world stage. What is clear, is that the unfortunate passing of Peter Carter is an event that has impacted Federer since the day it happened.

Gone But Not Forgotten

There were many people who were proud of Roger Federer the day he won Wimbledon for the first time in 2003. Adolf Kacovsky, the man who gave Roger his very first tennis lesson at The Old Boys Tennis Club in Basel, watched the final at the clubhouse with the rest of the current players and staff. He delightedly popped the champagne when Federer fell to his knees. Amongst the other proud onlookers, were Diana and Bob Carter, the parents of Peter Carter. They could see a little bit of Peter in Roger Federer whilst they watched him play that final. It helped massively with the loss of their son, who had died in a car crash less than a year before. When speaking of his victory after the match, he immediately paid homage to his former coach. "Peter was one of the most important people in my career. We would have had a big party together if he was still here. I'm sure he was watching it from somewhere", said an emotional Federer.[18]

Roger first heard the news of Carter's death when playing in Toronto, Canada. He came off court and was informed of the tragic event. He was completely shell-shocked. For a while after Peter's death, Federer couldn't concentrate on his tennis. He realised just how insignificant the game of tennis is when something like that happens. He pulled out of his next event and flew home to process what had happened. Of all the defeats on the court, nothing compared to the overwhelming grief of losing the man who helped him so much in his formative years. "I can never thank him enough for everything that he gave to me. Thanks to him I have my entire technique and coolness", confessed Federer.[17] There is no doubt that the death of Peter Carter made Federer stronger. It made him realise the immense talent he had, and how hard everybody had worked to get him to where he was, in particular his old coach. He made a decision after Carter's passing to dedicate himself entirely to his tennis, he was adamant he wouldn't let his talent go to waste. He felt he owed something to Carter, not achieving the heights he knew he could, would be seen as letting him down. He became calmer and more focused. He stopped letting his emotions get the better of him whilst on the court. It is no coincidence that less than 12 months after his passing, Federer went on to win Wimbledon. Even after his death, Carter was still having a positive influence. He was so much more than just a tennis coach, like so many great coaches are. He was a best friend, a mentor and somebody who acted like a big brother.[17]

In a way similar to Pete Sampras using the death of Tim Gullikson to help motivate him to reach his goals, it could be argued that Federer did the same. Research has suggested that athletes who have experienced tragedy in their personal lives often perform better under pressure than those who haven't.[26] Researchers from Nottingham Trent University, the University of Gloucestershire, South Wales, and Essex, found that exposure to negative life events can influence a person's cardiovascular system during high pressure moments. This higher cardiovascular activity helps to create better blood flow to the brain and muscles. The research team found that an athlete who had experienced a significant negative life event viewed difficult sporting situations as less demanding, or that they had the ability to overcome any obstacle put in their way.[26] It is therefore worth considering that after the passing of his former coach, Roger Federer gained a mental strength that he didn't have prior. The improvement in his game is certainly evidence of this. He began to focus more in matches, controlled his emotions better, and started to win more points in important moments. Despite this only being a theory, it's a reasonable debate to be had.

Roger Federer is now widely regarded as the best tennis player there has ever been. It's hard to argue with that when you look at his achievements and the way in which he effortlessly plays. It was The Old Boys Tennis Club that got him started however, and Roger will never forget his roots.

Table 2.1: Roger Federer Career Grand Slams by Year

2003	2004	2005	2006
Wimbledon	Wimbledon Australian Open U.S. Open	Wimbledon U.S. Open	Wimbledon Australian Open U.S. Open

2007	2008	2009	2010
Wimbledon Australian Open U.S. Open	U.S. Open	Wimbledon French Open	Australian Open

2012	2017	2018	
Wimbledon	Wimbledon Australian Open	Australian Open	

Chapter Three

The Spanish Revolution

"However great your dedication, you never win anything on your own".

Rafael Nadal

DURING THE 2017 SEASON, Toni Nadal announced that he would be stepping down as the coach of Rafael Nadal at the end of the year. The announcement was met with little attention, which may come as a surprise considering the major influence he has had not just on Rafa, but the rest of the tennis world. It was just the way Toni wanted it though. He isn't an individual to bring attention to himself, and he didn't want a huge media buzz surrounding his decision to leave the role as Rafa's head coach. By the time the pair parted ways in a professional sense, they had won more than 70 titles and over 850 matches together. An astounding record, and one that has seen Rafa become a legend of the sport. Whilst he gained world recognition for his talents, his coach has often remained an enigmatic figure.

Assigning the value of a tennis coach is a difficult task. You want to give credit where it's due, but at the same time you don't want to minimise the achievements of the person who is actually on the court, hitting the array of delightful shots and regularly doing all the winning. In Toni Nadal and Rafa, however, there is a fine medium. They are a duo who are mutually dependent on one another, whose strengths and weaknesses complement each other perfectly. It is without question that they are stronger together than they are alone. The influence of Uncle Toni on his nephew is profound, and it is well worth a chapter in this book.

The Nadal family is a fascinating one. There are many families over the course of history that have produced a couple of sporting stars. The Neville family in England comes to mind, with both Gary and Phil Neville playing football for Manchester United and England. Laila Ali and Muhammad Ali, the father and daughter combination, who were both professional boxers. Serena and Venus Williams too, both legends in the sport of tennis. But in the Nadal clan, they had produced a top-level professional footballer, and a record breaking professional tennis player within the space of a couple of decades. Now, that is far less common.

The father of the family, also named Rafael, surprisingly wasn't involved in sport at all. He was the conductor of the local orchestra in Manacor, a small town on the island of Mallorca, Spain, where the Nadal family have lived for centuries. He and his wife had five children. Four boys, named Sebastian, Rafael, Miguel and Toni, and one girl, named Marilen. All of the boys in the household, apart from Sebastian, were sport lovers. Miguel Nadal achieved the most success. After impressing whilst playing for his home club of Mallorca, Miguel was signed by FC Barcelona, where he went on to make over 200 appearances, and won five La Liga championships in an impressive career for the Catalan club. His brother, Toni, was a jack off all trades when it came to sport. He too played football, although not to the level of Miguel, and was also a Balearic Islands table tennis champion. He excelled the most however with his tennis. By the end of his tennis career, he could look back and proudly say that he was one of the best 30 tennis players in Spain at one point. His playing style was often very defensive and cagey, although extremely tactical. A trait you can often find in players who go on to become good coaches. He had excellent tactical nouse, and it was something he would end up passing to his nephew in years to come.[27] It was Sebastian Nadal, the least sporty of all the siblings, who without knowing it, changed the sport of tennis forever. When he and his wife Ana gave birth to their son on the 3rd of

June, 1986, they decided to name him Rafael Nadal after his grandfather. And just like that, a star was born.

The Code of Conduct

It was around the ages of three or four that Rafa Nadal held a tennis racquet for the first time. His Uncle Toni, who was now a coach at the Manacor tennis club, wanted his nephew to start early. Almost immediately, Toni was impressed by the power and ferocity of Rafa. He played tennis the same way his uncle Miguel played football for Barcelona years earlier, aggressively and without fear.[27] Almost from the get go, time ceased to exist for a young Rafa whenever he played tennis. Most of the younger players at the club would play for a while and get bored. They'd put their racquets down and go and watch football instead. But that wasn't the case for Toni's nephew. He's a self confessed lover of football, but whilst out on the court playing, he simply couldn't get enough. He would play until he was completely satisfied. Even without being told, he'd work on any weaknesses he had. Rafa seemed to have a real streak of competitiveness in him, always wanting to play and beat the older kids who were bigger and stronger. Even at such a tender age, he had enormous discipline to coincide with his organic talent and desire to win.[27]

Toni's advice to his nephew, right from the very beginning,

was simple. In a way similar to that of Jack Nicklaus, when he said golf is all about hitting the ball far to begin with, and then focusing on getting it in the hole, Toni said something similar. "First, hit the ball hard; then we'll see about keeping it in". Those were perhaps the very first coaching tips Rafa Nadal ever heard.[28] It's different to how many other coaches first begin to teach their students. Control of the ball is often the initial focus of any practice session, not power. But Toni saw the game differently.

It's not uncommon for coaches to give family members special treatment when it comes to behaviour and discipline. Whether it's football, tennis, basketball, or any other sport, the manager or coach can often be seen giving that extra bit of leniency to their child, or nephew or whatever the case may be. You hear countless stories of players only being in the football team because 'their father is the manager', however true or untrue that may be. It could not have been any more different for Rafa Nadal when he was first starting out at the Manacor tennis club with his uncle.[28] Whether he was in the presence of his friends or not, Toni immediately coached with an intention of constructing an inner toughness to Rafa. He would receive no special treatment whatsoever. You could often see the youngster, whilst the rest of the boys at the club had left, sweeping the courts and picking all the balls up after a practice session under the orders of his uncle. Despite being by far and out a better player than the rest of the kids his age, Toni was keen to nullify any arrogance in Rafa before it began to emerge. "Just because you are good at hitting tennis balls, that makes you no better or worse than anybody else", he would say.[27] If the two of them were having a private session together, Toni would always stand on the side of the court where the sun beamed down, leaving Rafa to train in the shade. Another method Toni used to toughen up his nephew was with the tennis balls. When starting to practice, Toni would make sure they had plenty of good, and often new, balls. Suddenly, he would feed an old lifeless, dead ball that wouldn't bounce and would shoot off in a random direction. Rafa was taught to never, ever complain. "The balls might be third rate", he would say, "but you are fourth rate!"[28] Perhaps the thing that riled Rafa up the most was when they played matches with each other. When training, the pair would play a match up to 20. Toni would let Rafa get to within one point of winning. The youngster wouldn't be able to contain his excitement, thinking that was the day he would finally beat his uncle. As soon as Rafa got to 19, Toni would instantly up his game, getting to 20 points before his nephew. It was very much a cruel to be kind way of coaching. There was a deeper reasoning behind all this, however. Toni was teaching Rafa the principle of endurance. How to continue no matter what. At such a young age he was being taught how to be resilient, how not to give up after disappointment or when things seem unfair.[28] To coincide with this, Toni set out very specific ground rules for Rafa, rules that he must absolutely follow:[27]

*

I. If you ever throw a racquet, we're finished. They're expensive, and when you throw a racquet you don't just disrespect the sport, you disrespect all the people who can't afford equipment.

II. Losing is part of competing. You will lose. And when you lose, it's not going to be my fault or the fault of your racquet or the balls or the courts or the weather. It is your fault, and you will accept it. Too many people in this world make excuses for their problems. You take responsibility and try and do better next time. That's all.

III. Have fun. When you stop enjoying this, it's no good. You'll find something else that gives you pleasure.

These ground rules that Toni put into effect at the Manacor tennis club perfectly aligned with the way in which he believed children should be taught on the tennis court. Toni didn't agree with how youngsters often behaved. "The problem is that too much effort is invested in boosting their self-esteem. They are therefore made to feel special, without having done anything. People get confused: they fail to grasp that you are not special because of who you are but because of what you do". Toni was wary of his nephew becoming spoiled. He knew Rafa had immense talent, and after just a few years of training him there was an inkling that Rafa could go far in the game of tennis. He was determined to make sure that if Rafa did go on to make some money from the sport and achieve fame, he would keep his feet firmly on the ground. If he was going to become a star, he was going to be an incredibly humble one. The world humble doesn't sit particularly well with Toni, though. "He just knows his place in the world", he said.[28]

Whilst Rafa possessed incredible natural ability, it wasn't the way he played on court that his uncle prioritised originally. He looked beyond the talent, and instead focused on the type of person he wanted to see on the tennis court when he watched his young nephew play. He wanted to see somebody who expressed themselves and showed their personality, but in no way was a show-off or a diva. He felt there were too many of those already in the game of tennis. Roger Federer was perhaps heading in that direction before Peter Carter came into his life. It was far more important for Toni that Rafa first of all became a good person before he became a good player. Being well mannered in defeat and gracious in victory. Respectful to the umpires, and as he progressed, the fans too. You would struggle to look back at any of Rafa's matches throughout his career, unlike that of Roger, and find footage of him acting childish or displaying any form of negative outburst. Toni knew he could be harder on Rafa than the other kids because he could not only take it, but thrive off it. When he eventually started playing tournaments, Rafa knew not to complain. Whether he had a crack in the frame of his racquet that was causing issues, had a difficult day at school, or had a slight injury. Any complaints wouldn't sit well with his coach.

Slowly but surely, Toni was building a warrior. Someone who knew how not only to endure suffering, but to enjoy it.[28]

At a tournament in Terrassa, a town not far from Barcelona, Rafa arrived with his uncle and another player from the Manacor club who had also entered. As luck would have it, they had to play their opening games at the same time on different courts. To avoid any favouritism, Toni decided to watch Rafa from afar, standing in an area that meant he could follow both games simultaneously. Although stood a fair distance from Rafa, he could perfectly see what was going on. His nephew was having a disaster. His serving was off, he was missing simple shots and overall making a real mess of the match. It made little sense. His opponent was somebody who Rafa was expected to beat quite comfortably, so it was obvious he was playing badly rather than being outplayed. At 6-1 down, a friend of Toni's walked over and spoke to him.[29]

"Toni, doesn't your nephew have another racquet?" asked his friend.

"Yes, of course he does. Why?"

"I think he's playing with a broken racquet".

Toni immediately ran over to Rafa's court, taking full advantage of the break in between the first and second set. "Rafael, I think you're playing with a broken racquet. Look at it, let's see", enquired Toni. Rafa picked his racquet up off the floor, he had no idea what his uncle was talking about. "Yikes! It's broken", he replied. Toni immediately handed Rafa another racquet, and he walked back onto court ready for the second set.[29] After losing the first set comfortably, he won the second set 7-5 and played far better for the rest of the match. Clearly, his damaged racquet was a major factor in his poor first set performance. Toni, feeling somewhat perplexed, approached Rafa after the match and asked him how after all his years of playing tennis, he wasn't able to notice that he was playing with a splintered frame. Whether you're somebody who plays tennis once a year, or somebody who plays every single day, you'll know that playing tennis with a broken frame is virtually impossible. Shots will fly all over the place, resulting in very little control. Rafa replied with the only way he knew. "Toni, I am so used to being to blame for everything that it never occurred to me that the thing responsible for my bad game was the racquet. I thought I was the one doing it wrong".[29] A brilliant response. That match almost poetically exemplified Rafa's state of mind. Toni's advice actually back-fired in that first set, although that was very rare it must be said.

Two-Handed Forehands

In regards to his on court playing style, his early technique was extremely peculiar. A lot of the work done by Toni, as we have seen, was based on attitude and temperament. Subsequently, Rafa played with a style that was somewhat lacking behind his other friends at the tennis club. He certainly knew how to hit the ball hard, and was slowly starting to place more of his shots inside the lines of the court, but there was something different about the way Rafa hit his shots.[27]

Until the age of eight, Rafa used two hands to hit his forehand, and two hands to hit his backhand. This is unheard of. Usually, as soon as a youngster starts playing tennis, even at the age of four or five, they're shown the basic principles. You use one hand for your forehand, and one or two for the backhand. But in no coaching manual would you find a page that tells you to use two hands to hit a forehand. Perhaps it was genius on the part of Toni. Rafa would often fire balls right past his opponents in practice using this technique. It certainly helped to build his confidence, despite onlookers looking on in bemusement. One day however, not long after Rafa's 8th birthday, Toni decided to make the transition.[27]

"I always hated playing against lefties" confessed Toni.[27] Whilst his nephew was predominantly ambidextrous, using his right hand to do pretty much everything, he noticed that when playing football, he tended to use his left foot more. Playing every shot with two hands in his early years had actually helped Rafa. He would just use one hand to hold the racquet but the other to guide the ball, so he was essentially playing forehands on both sides despite it appearing he was playing purely backhands. There are many advantages to playing tennis left-handed. Not only does it mean firing your trusty forehands to an opponent's usually weaker backhand, but it also means being able to open the court with ease when serving on the advantage side. This means that in around 75 per-cent of all the possible situations in a close match, a left-handed player will gain a slight edge by serving on their favoured side. This probably explains Toni's hatred of playing against them throughout his career. In a very brief conversation that would go on to change the course of tennis history, Toni told Rafa that from now on he would play left-handed. As usual, he nodded, accepted what Toni had said, and got to work.[27]

It wasn't long after that conversation that Rafa was smashing left-handed forehand winners, and serving brilliantly with his off-hand too. His sling-shot like approach to hitting shots that he had been playing with all of his life was working even better with his new and improved, more contemporary technique. A few months later, with of course plenty of on court practicing, Toni witnessed his young nephew become the champion of Spain in his age group at around the age of nine. A fantastic achievement, and one that confirmed everybody's thoughts on the ability of the young boy from Mallorca. No surprise however, his uncle didn't let it go to his head. After winning the tournament, he pulled Rafa to one side and asked him to read the list of previous winners to see if he recognised any of them. As to be expected, he could name barely one, if any. Uncle Toni wanted Rafa to learn that winning that tournament and becoming the best in his country, whilst despite being a magnificent accomplishment, did not guarantee success.[27] Toni was in no way going to let it get to Rafa's head. There was still plenty of work to be done if his nephew was to become a top player. Evidence of this can be seen throughout that tournament, and many others that Rafa participated in around that time. Whenever he had played a fantastic match or hit a brilliant shot, Toni would reply with something along the lines of, 'that was good, but your volleying needs some work'. There were definitely times it frustrated Rafa, but it always seemed to push him, his uncle's words encouraged him to continuously improve.[27] There was one time, however, when it appeared Toni had taken it too far with the treatment of his nephew.

After a training session at the Manacor tennis club with his uncle, Rafa, who has admitted to not being very naturally coordinated, tried to jump over the net. It ended disastrously. His foot caught the top of the net and he spectacularly flew through the air, landing directly on his arm. The 13-year-old had badly sprained his wrist, much to the outrage of his coach. "You, Rafael, you have got nothing inside your head!" he bellowed, offering no sympathy. Rafa's godfather took him to the hospital, and was furious with the way Toni had treated his godson. Crucially, it was this moment that made a teenage Rafa realise he could go one of two ways. He could either side with his godfather and rebel against the way his uncle coached and treated him, or side with his uncle instead. By the age of 13, Rafa had his eyes firmly set on becoming a champion in the sport of tennis, and he knew his best way of getting there was by having his uncle by his side. The ongoing list of harsh lessons that Toni had taught Rafa gave him the skill set to eventually thrive as a professional tennis player, and even at the time, Rafa knew that.[28] As soon as his arm healed, he was back on court with his uncle.

The work the pair were doing on the court was propelling Rafa onto the world stage at an impressively quick rate. By the time the young prodigy was 15, he was already a professional tennis player and competing at major tournaments. His god given talent coincided with Toni's ability to distinguish the lines between learning and training. He had passed on as much off court knowledge as on court knowledge. He efficiently used his incredible ability of transmitting technical, tactical, and mental understanding to a young Rafa, giving him the platform to improve on them all through their training on the court.[30] He was becoming an extremely rounded player in all aspects, and the world was starting to take notice. It was a tournament just before he turned professional however, at age 14, that Rafa still points out to this day as being one he will always remember.[28]

It was not long after the incident with Rafa's godfather and the sprained wrist, that everything the pair had worked on emphatically came together. The tournament was held in Madrid, around 500 miles from Manacor. Rafa had entered the tournament the year before, but was knocked out in the semi-final. He and Toni made it their mission to win the tournament this time around, with another year of practice under their belt, and another 12 months of Rafa growing physically, too. In the first round, the youngster from Manacor fell and broke his little finger. It wouldn't have been a stupid idea to pull out and avoid any further damage, but Rafa knew that with his uncle's vigilant eye watching over him, that wasn't going to happen. He knew not to complain. He ended the match with victory and moved onto the next round. Rafa decided not to bandage his little finger either, as doing so would have made it harder to hit the ball effectively. Instead, he would use only four fingers, leaving the broken 'pinky' finger to dangle off the edge of the handle. It wasn't too difficult to hit backhands, as most of the weight shifted to his right hand, taking pressure off his left where the broken finger was. Forehands however, particularly the forehand drive, one of his most brilliant shots, was agonising. Every shot would end in a shooting pain that seemed to spread right up his arm. Nevertheless, in true Rafa style, he gritted his teeth and battled his way through to the final.

In the final, he met his good friend and somebody who he still hits with today, Toméu Salva. A tough opponent, and somebody who was incredibly hard to beat when in full heath, never mind with a broken finger. The years and years of harsh lessons and cruel to be kind coaching paid off in that final. Rafa forgot about the pain, he didn't consider complaining for one second. He played an incredible match and beat his friend Salva 6-4 in the third and final set. It was the images after the match that proved significant, and was a measure of how hard Rafa had battled. The pain once the match had ended was so severe, he couldn't even lift the trophy. If you look at the photo from the end of the match, another boy is helping him lift the winner's trophy up for the photographs. Incredible. Rafa was an armour plated warrior even before he'd become a pro. Toni was proud of Rafa that day, he'd become the player he always wanted him to be. Rafa often said that it was harder to practice with his uncle than it was to play a final, so the way he fought to success in that tournament should perhaps come as little surprise.[31] He himself takes inspiration from the hurdles he overcame when he was younger. "I look back at that teenage Rafael and I am proud of him. He set a benchmark of endurance that has served me as an example and as a reminder ever since that you can put mind over matter, and if you want something badly enough, no sacrifice is too great", he confessed years later.[28]

Decisions

It was around the time of that tournament that Rafa had a decision to make regarding his coaching. As mentioned earlier, by the age of 14, Rafa had already started to gain the attention of huge brands like Nike and Adidas, with sports companies desperate to sign the young warrior to their books. It wasn't just sponsors either. Tennis academies up and down the country were keen for him to join them, none more so perhaps, than the High Performance Centre of San Cugat. The academy, which is situated in Barcelona, not far from Rafa's hometown, had offered him a scholarship. This was significant in a number of ways. Not only would he be able to work under the tutelage of world class coaches and train with other top quality players of a similar age, it would also be completely free. The academy in San Cugat was, at the time, the best in Europe, and Rafa had a huge decision on his hands. In a way similar to Roger Federer years prior, Rafa had to decide if he should stick with the coach who had been with him since the beginning, or cut ties and join a top training academy.

Unlike that of Federer, Nadal chose to stay in Manacor and continue to train with his uncle. "I wanted to stay at home, work with my uncle and keep my family around me", confessed Rafa.[28] There was a fear amongst the Nadal family at the time that Rafa could easily lose his bearings in Barcelona at the academy, or worse, let his success get to his head. After all, leaving Toni's watchful eye would increase the possibility of Rafa losing his incredible level-headiness that had seen him become the player he was. It was a feature of his game that set him apart from other players his age, and something that had been drilled into him since the start by his uncle. To lose that would have been catastrophic. Rafa was blissfully aware that as frustrating as Toni was at times, he would never be able to find a better coach or mentor. In a decision that shifted away from the norm, Rafa continued working with his uncle, rather than move away and let somebody else take control of his coaching.

It was a commitment that Rafa has never looked back on with an ounce of regret. "I don't know if, at that time, I would have been mentally prepared to go and train and live somewhere else", he recalled.[32] "Success might have gone to my head in Barcelona; it never would with Toni or my family around, all of whom conspired to keep me grounded".[28] Uncle Toni was as good as any other top coach in bringing out the best in Rafa on the court through practicing, but what set him apart was the way he could influence him off it. Tennis came easy to Rafa, his uncle was a master in making sure nothing else did.[27]

When all the top brands were vying for Rafa's endorsement, he was sent some free trainers to try by Nike and Reebok. Money was never a real issue for the Nadal clan, his decision not to take a free scholarship and continue training with his uncle was evidence of that. When they received those free trainers from Nike and Reebok however, everybody was excited, and treated them with the utmost respect. There was one incident that gave a perfect example of their regard to everyone and everything. When leaving for practice, Rafa didn't bother untying the laces of his new free trainers, instead, he forced his foot into them, wriggling his toes until his foot slid in, bending the heel in the process. As to be expected, his uncle was furious. "You untie them and put them on properly and show respect. They may not cost you anything, but that doesn't mean they're not expensive," his uncle shouted.[28] It's safe to say Rafa doesn't force his feet into his trainers anymore, another strong lesson from his uncle.

That same year, Rafa qualified for a tournament in South Africa. He had won a series of tournaments in his native Spain, sponsored by Nike (the sponsor he eventually chose), and in doing so he had qualified for the grand final. It was the final of the Nike Junior Tour International, where the winners from all the other tournaments in different countries gathered to play against one another. Nadal went over representing Spain. South Africa was by far the furthest Rafa had ever been away from home to compete. Toni was unsure whether Rafa should go, he again was wary of his nephew becoming overly sure of himself. He put that to one side however, as playing in South Africa would offer valuable experience; competing against the world's best foreign players his age, and would of course give Rafa an insight as to what it is like to be a professional tennis player on the tour. The tournament would also be one of Rafa's only without his uncle by his side. It was another coach and close family friend, Jofre Porta, who would travel with Rafa instead. Toni's phobia of flying was one of the main reasons for the decision, with 12 hours of air time not especially on his list of favourite things to do.

Whilst out there, Rafa acted with a freedom he perhaps couldn't when Toni was around. He smashed forehand topspin winners and lethal backhands as he progressed to the final. It was on the morning of the final that Rafa did something he wouldn't have dreamt about doing if his uncle Toni was there. He played football for two hours. The organisers, somewhat baffled and infuriated by what they were watching, appealed to

Jofre, asking him to stop Rafa from playing, feeling as though their tournament was being outrageously disrespected. In a brilliant moment however, Jofre refused, and let Rafa continue playing. Knowing he was going against the orders of Toni, he reminded everybody that travelling across the world at such a tender age to play tennis has to be fun. If you take the fun out of it, it wouldn't be long before Rafa lost his passion for the game.[28] Profound words, and it was this moment that made Rafa realise he could still have fun and compete at the same time.

After winning the tournament, Rafa arrived home the next day. His grandparents had put congratulatory banners out, and placed balloons all over the house to celebrate his incredible victory in South Africa. Rafa never got to see those celebrations. Toni, upon seeing the new decorations around the house, was furious. He met Rafa at the door to the house before he got inside. "You can go home now. I'll come along after I've given your grandparents a talking to". Rafa couldn't believe it. He'd won one of the biggest tournaments of his life, and it appeared his uncle's overriding feeling was anger rather than joy. Toni was worried that all the success would go to Rafa's head. He was determined not to give what Rafa had achieved much importance in another attempt to keep his feet on the ground. It didn't end there, either. Toni drove over to Rafa's house later on, and told him in no uncertain terms he should be ready and waiting at 9 a.m. the next morning to train. Rafa was furious of course, he'd just won in South

Africa, had just landed after a 12 hour flight, and now his uncle was telling him they must train the following morning at 9 a.m. Feeling incredibly mistreated, Nadal rebelled and said he wouldn't be there. But of course, the following morning, despite being in a foul mood, he was ready and waiting to train with his uncle at 9 a.m. sharp.[28]

On Court Improvements

To coincide with the off court lessons Rafa had been taught, his on court training was progressing, too. As Rafa found himself on the cusp of becoming a professional, his uncle's training methods began to show their worth.

Toni recalls asking Rafa how far he wanted to go in the sport of tennis a few years before he turned professional. "If you want to become the Manacor champion, or the champion of Mallorca, we have already trained enough", he said. If Rafa was happy to look back in years to come and be content at being the champion of his small town, he could go home and relax as the work was already done, according to his uncle. "If you want to be the champion of Spain, however, we have to train more", declared Toni to his nephew. Of course Rafa wanted more out of tennis than just to have the champion of Manacor on his list of achievements, and it was at this point Toni slightly adjusted his coaching methods.[29]

During their training sessions, he would be very incisive in setting clear aims and objectives at the start of each practice. In doing so, it encouraged Rafa to think on his own, and to understand how much he had left to do if he was to become an elite tennis player. One of Toni's main principles was making sure Rafa entered the practice court every single day with a set objective. He wouldn't train with Rafa for the sake of training, there was always a deeper meaning or target that they intended to achieve come the end of the session. Every time Rafa stepped on court to practice, the youngster had in his mind what he had to do. To coincide with this, Toni confessed that Rafa always worked hard. "If physical problems didn't prevent him, he has worked seriously hard in all of our workouts". By making sure Rafa set the goals himself before each session, it ensured that Rafa was self-demanding and didn't simply do what he was told by his coach. It enabled him to make important decisions in matches without having to be told to do so by anybody else. Toni would also take advantage of the time they spent in the car together, with the duo often spending hours driving to and from practice and tournaments. They would talk about what they needed to improve, the type of intensity the pair needed to input into their training, and the importance of giving 100 per-cent in every session. "In purely tennis terms, I always tried to let him make the decisions, so that he himself knows how to perceive the action appropriate to the challenge".[29]

As prior mentioned, it's common for coaches to plan

set drills with their players and repeat them. The footwork sessions that Peter Lundgren used with Federer is an example of that, or the blocked-style of coaching that Sampras used with Joe Brandi. For Toni though, he was never a fan of repeat patterns of practice. A further downside of repeated drills is that it discourages the player to make proactive decisions. With Rafa, he wanted his nephew to make decisions at his own discretion. For example, he would ask Rafa to hit with another player, but tell him that for the next ten minutes he must go to the net and hit volleys, the more times the better. He didn't want to tell Rafa when to go forward and hit a volley, he wanted Rafa to work out for himself when he should race to the net and hit the shot. By training this way, Toni transferred the decision making from coach to student. The drill wasn't repeated or orchestrated, and it forced Rafa to think for himself.[29]

This type of practice even transferred into Rafa's matches, too. Around the age of 14, he played in the Mallorca Tournament in his hometown. Whilst being an excellent player on the verge of playing tennis full-time, Toni recognised that his nephew's game needed work if he was to excel on the professional circuit. On the way to the tournament, he asked Rafa to get to the net as often as possible and use his volley. Slightly confused, Rafa agreed. Toni knew that by asking him to do this, he was greatly narrowing Rafa's chances of winning that match as his volley was the weakest part of his game. He knew, however, that asking Rafa to use that tactic was necessary at that moment to promote learning from him. Toni understood that sometimes we have to put aside what is good for us to win a match at that particular moment, in pursuit of learning for the greater good. Short term pain for long term gain. As expected, Rafa lost the match. On the way home, Rafa mentioned that if he hadn't gone to the net so many times, he'd have probably won the match, and Toni agreed. What was pivotal here, though, was that Rafa learned his need to improve his volleying on his own. He'd been on court in a tournament and lost, and it was because of his weak volleying. Rafa, when realising he was going to lose the match if he continued playing that way, could have easily forgotten what his uncle had told him and disregarded his volley for the remainder of the game. He didn't, however, and above all, he didn't get carried away with his desire to win. He had shown commitment to his coach, and by doing so had learned a valuable lesson.[29]

Toni knew that the duo had to continue improving. Not just Rafa, but himself as a coach too. Whether his nephew had become the champion of his town, or later the champion of Roland-Garros, their work was never complete. Toni always made a conscious effort to make sure Rafa walked away from every practice with some degree of dissatisfaction. Even after a highly impressive training session, once the pair were sitting, analysing how they thought it had gone, after talking about the positives, Toni would emphasise on the things that needed to be improved upon slightly more. Rafa always went home with a very clear idea of what he had to improve for the following session. No matter how fantastic a player he was becoming, he always knew exactly what to work on next.[29]

Battling With Roger

In the year 2006, Rafa and Roger Federer faced one another six times. They met in Dubai, Rome, Monte Carlo, the Masters Cup, the French Open final and the Wimbledon Final.

The Monte Carlo Masters final, played at the Monte Carlo Country Club, is surprisingly not situated in Monte Carlo, or even Monaco for that matter. The prestigious clay court tennis club can actually be found in the Alpes-Maritimes department of France, just outside Monaco's northeastern border. In 2006, it hosted a final played between the two men aforementioned. Federer, at the time, was at the height of his powers. Ranked as the number one player in the world, he was somebody admired by the tennis world, none more so perhaps than Toni and Rafa Nadal. Roger was on course that year to win more Grand Slam titles than suffer defeats. He'd won every Grand Slam more than once at that stage of his career, aside from the French Open, and was a heavy favourite to win any tournament he entered, Grand Slam or not.

The Spaniard was also no pushover when the pair met in that final. He was fresh off winning the French Open almost 12 months earlier, and had pushed Federer, the king of grass, to four sets in the Wimbledon final earlier in the season. It was billed as a dream final in France that year, but that wasn't how uncle Toni saw it.

Rafa went into the tournament as the reigning champion, having beaten an excellent clay court player in Argentina's Guillermo Coria in three sets the year before. He was determined to achieve the ultimate prize in back to back years. The tournament got off to the best possible start. He was pitted against former French Davis Cup captain Arnaud Clément in the first round, a match he won comfortably in straight sets. He played Jean-René Lisnard, Kristof Vliegan, and the previous year's final opponent, Guillermo Coria, in the subsequent matches. All were beaten without dropping a set. The semi-final proved to be little challenge to Rafa, either. He beat Argentinian Gastón Gaudio in three sets, 5-7, 6-1, 6-1 to reach the final, where Roger Federer awaited. His Swiss opponent had also only dropped a singular set, with the multiple Grand Slam winner losing a set to a very young qualifier by the name of Novak Djokovic. The stage was set. Toni and Rafa began their preparations for the final.[29]

Just like before every match Rafa and Toni prepared for, they spent the best part of an hour discussing the game plan. They knew it was going to be tough. Despite Rafa's dominance on clay, Roger always presented a tough obstacle to overcome. To become the best player in the world, both Rafa and Toni knew that he was the man to beat, not just in the upcoming final, but in the coming years.[29] It wasn't long before Rafa asked his uncle a question on how he thought the game would go. What

Toni replied I don't think anybody expected. In a way similar to that of their days at the Manacor tennis club, Toni provided a harsh answer. "Well, lets see", he bluntly replied. "Federer has a better drive than you. His reverse is also better than yours. The volley, much better. The smash, better than yours...".[29] Just as Toni was about to go into specifics regarding how much better Federer's serve was to that of his nephew's, Rafa interrupted. "Stop! Stop!", he had heard enough. In typical Toni fashion however, there was a deeper meaning behind his unflattering spiel. He wanted his nephew to go out onto court with a fire inside of him. He was aware of the challenge ahead, and needed Rafa to be absolutely committed to the cause if they were to stand a chance of victory. "Look, Rafael. What I am telling you is the truth. If you want, I can deceive you and tell you that you are better than him. But don't worry, Federer is not going to fool you, and when you take to the court in an hour, he will tell you the same as me". Toni was squeezing Rafa, but not choking him. It was a tactic used countless times over the course of their professional relationship.[29] When he began his speech regarding Federer's technical dominance, he had already planned what he was going to say next. He explained to his nephew that despite all that, he could beat Roger in attitude. "Against his tennis superiority, there is little you can do. But you can beat him with your desire".[29] He wanted Rafa to play every single point as though it was the last point he would ever play. He knew that if Rafa played his best tennis, and matched that with unrivalled attitude and a relentless desire to win, he could come out on top. As to be expected, he walked onto court for the final with the ambition of making Federer work for every single point. You'd have been a foolish person to doubt his chances of victory that day if you had heard the discussion between him and his uncle just an hour prior. Sports psychology has significantly improved tennis coaching at all levels of the game, particularly at the top end. The technical and physical abilities of the top twenty or thirty players in the world are remarkably similar. If you were to look back at the career of Rafa Nadal and Roger Federer for example, the hours they had each spent on court practicing would most probably add up to a similar number. This, in turn, means psychological skills take on even greater importance to gain a competitive edge.[11] Despite the general agreement amongst those involved in tennis of the importance of mental attributes, a large number of coaches are inconsistent in implementing them into a player's daily training schedule.[11] Like the technical side of the game, mental skills need to be practiced regularly, and Toni Nadal was a firm believer in this. He would always find the right words to challenge his nephew, ensuring he regularly took to the court with the right state of mind.

As the two men walked out, the crowd, unsurprisingly, couldn't wait for the action to begin. Rafa's style of play suited the surface at the Monte Carlo Country Club. Clay courts are perfect for players who tend to play towards the defensive side of the spectrum. If your conditioning is good, too, it helps. The ball bounces much higher on clay than on other surfaces, which in turn means players have more time to react and get the ball back. You'll often see brilliantly long rallies when watching a clay court tournament, with both players firing shots back and forth at one another. Mentally, it can take its toll. Matches can go on for extraordinarily long periods of time. A five hour match at the French Open for example is a common theme. Each point is a battle, it's virtually impossible to smash winners past the person on the other side of the net without having orchestrated the point effectively beforehand. You have to build, slowly forcing your opponent out of position by hitting wide angled shots before you realistically have a chance of hitting a ground-stroke that's nonreturnable. Perhaps it's all these factors added together that make Rafa a simply magnificent clay court player. His insane ability to turn defence into attack in an instant coincides with his mental toughness and endurance, creating a perfect mix of ingredients for playing on the the deep red surface. Whilst Roger was perhaps the favourite when both players woke up that morning of the final, did he really ever have a chance?

The final itself was one of the most entertaining and fascinating matches the pair had played at that point in their great rivalry. The match was just shy of four hours. Three hours and fifty minutes to be precise. To the delight of his uncle, Rafa lifted the trophy, beating the world number one in four sets.

At the start of the match, Rafa came racing out of the blocks, with his uncle's words still ringing in his ears. For Roger, however, the first set started auspiciously. Before you could blink, Rafa had broken serve twice and found himself 4-0 up. It took 42 minutes for Rafa to wrap up the first set 6-2. He had a point to prove to his uncle, and in his head, there was no way he was losing.

Roger, using all his experience and outright talent, wasn't going down without a fight. After losing the first set, he hit back and claimed the second set for himself after a 7-2 win in the tie-breaker, to pull it back to 1-1. It was here on out however, that Rafa started to get the better of Roger in all the crucial moments. After breaking Rafa early in third set, Roger had another game point. Somehow, Roger hit one of the worst shots of his career, even to this day. His smash landed way out of the court. It's a shot the man from Switzerland would make 99 times out of 100. From that point on, the match belonged to Toni's nephew. He fought back from a number of break points, broke Federer's serve on countless occasions, and never allowed his opponent to win a singular easy point. A delicious forehand winner flew past Federer to hand the Spaniard the match. At 19 years of age, the boy from Manacor was becoming a serious problem for Roger Federer. 6-2, 6-7, 6-3, 7-6. He had retained his crown in Monte Carlo, and his victory never looked in doubt. Under his uncle's gazing eyes, Nadal had become the most exciting player in the world, and the duo had the world number one spot firmly in their sights. Federer had found himself in a very strange predicament of having lost the same number of matches halfway through the season in 2006, than he did the entirety of the 2005 season. One thing stood out more than any other. All of his losses had come to the same person. Rafael Nadal. Roger was ranked the best player in the world, but he just couldn't seem to beat the world number two.

The rivalry perhaps reached its climax not long after the match in Monte Carlo. Half way through the final in Rome, a tournament that Rafa dominated, Roger appeared frustrated. For a while, there was a feeling amongst those on the tour that Rafa was getting away with more than he should whilst on court. Players were starting to get annoyed with Toni Nadal in particular, and how he appeared to get away with coaching Rafa throughout matches, which is categorically not allowed. As Federer reached the baseline before partaking in the next point, he looked to Rafa's coach and uttered the words, "alright, Toni". It was perhaps Roger's gentleman like approach of telling Rafa's uncle to shut up. Whether Toni was actually coaching Rafa through matches or not remains unclear, but during that battle in 2006, it certainly appeared to grind on Roger.[17] The rivalry between the pair was very much an on court battle rather than off, as the two players have always been good friends and hugely respectful of one another.

*

The Australian Open

Toni Nadal has often stated that his nephew is probably the best tennis player at winning matches when playing badly.[29] That is testament to the resilience and extremely hard working nature of Rafa, instilled in him from a young age by his coach. The Spaniard understands that it is impossible to consistently be 100 per-cent when doing anything in life, let alone elite sport. Aforementioned, playing perfect tennis everyday is impossible, no matter who you are or how long you have been playing for. Perhaps one of Rafa's greatest traits taught by Toni, is the ability to understand that a rival player can play better than you on a particular day, and that it is completely natural. When an opponent is playing better tennis than Rafa, he doesn't accept that as a reason to collapse and accept defeat. He creates another opportunity for himself by overcoming adversity with a never say die spirit, and the mental attributes that he had worked on with his coach.[29] By the year 2009, the duo had developed a number of on court routines that Rafa implemented regularly in between points and changeovers. The most noticeable was perhaps the activation strategies used before the start of each match. He would - and still does - use short, sharp movements and high jumps whilst the umpire tosses a coin to decide who wants to serve first. Following this, he sprints towards the back of the court at lightning pace. Not only does this improve body stiffness, it can help towards concentration and focus.[11] By following a mental routine before the game has started, as well as taking more time in between serves to stable himself, Rafa has been able to achieve a relaxed state throughout certain moments, which have proved crucial over the course of his career.

The semi-final of the Australian Open that year pitted Rafa against his compatriot, Fernando Verdasco, and those inside the Rod Laver Stadium were treated to a remarkable spectacle. Rafa came up against an extremely hard working player in scin-tillating form. Verdasco had eliminated Britain's Andy Murray in the fourth round, and followed that up with a brilliant win over Frenchman Jo-Wilfried Tsonga in the quarter-final. No Spanish player had won the Australian Open before, but in 2009, the two Spaniards made up 50 per-cent of the semi-final draw, with Roger Federer and Andy Roddick competing in the other half.

The match was like no other. It swung one way, and then the other, with three out of the five sets going to a tie-break. Both players' physical and mental endurance was pushed to the limit in that match. Five hours and fourteen minutes of tennis was played before it saw an eventual winner. At the time, it was the longest Grand Slam match ever played, although beaten the following year at Wimbledon, in a match that lasted 11 hours and over three days by John Isner and Nicholas Mahut. Verdasco, who had multiple years of experience over his fellow Spaniard, possessed amazing physical strength, which was perhaps at its most ruthless peak throughout the tournament.

The semi-final was one of those matches that lived long in the memory of those that witnessed it. The never say die attitude of both men meant points lasted an age, leaving the crowd breathless, and the coaches and family members of the players' almost unable to watch. Uncle Toni was on the verge of collapse, let alone Rafa! The match could have easily gone either way, but the final set fell in favour of the 22-year-old from Manacor. By the end of the bout, both players were lifeless, having given every inch of what they had, leaving nothing on the court. The crowd of course were enthralled at what they had just witnessed. With Roger Federer defeating Roddick in the other semi-final, Rafa had less than 48 hours to recover.

The Swiss had already emerged victorious at the Australian Open on three occasions before he made it to the final in 2009. He beat Russian Marat Safin in straight sets in 2004, Marcos Baghdatis in 2006, and followed that up with victory over Fernando González in 2007. In the eyes of the public, and that of the experts', Roger was favourite to reign supreme in Melbourne once again in 2009. A few hours before Rafa and Roger were due to walk onto court for the final, it appeared those in the Nadal camp felt victory was more of a dream than a reality too.[29]

Despite the efforts of his physio and the rest of Rafa's team to nurture him back to full health, the recovery time between the semi-final and the final was too short. The previous match against Verdasco had required such an almighty effort, it had left him both mentally and physically exhausted. On the morning of the final, Toni's worst fears were confirmed.[29] Just like before all the finals Rafa had played in, he along with his coach and the rest of his team, entered the practice court with the ambition of having a light session. "We entered the court ready to train smoothly, to touch the ball, to look for positive feelings, and what we found was just the opposite", confessed Toni.[29] It was clear from Rafa's face that he was in pain. His arms, his hip, his knee. Everything was in agony. He'd hit for a short while and experience dizziness and cramping. There was a real sense of panic and helplessness amongst the Nadal camp that morning. Toni knew he had to do something. He had helped his nephew overcome many obstacles throughout his career so far, but this without doubt the biggest yet. Rafa could barely hit a tennis ball, and was just hours away from playing against Roger Federer in the Australian Open final.

The day of the final was not about practicing or working on specific drills. It was about providing the right words to give Rafa the mental push he needed. Toni began with his vocal encouragement. "Come on, Rafael, you are going to play the final of the Australian Open. Make an effort; the last effort".[29] His on court movements continued to be jaded, overcome with pain. Toni didn't let up, though. He continued to stand by the side of Rafa, nagging him constantly. In unusual style, his nephew responded assertively: "Sure, Toni, it's very easy for you".[29] After all, it was Rafa who had taken part in that epic semi-final match, not his uncle. It's easy for somebody else to stand there and tell you to make the effort when they're in full health. This didn't deter Toni from his tactic of trying to motivate his nephew. "Of course it's not easy. But you will probably never have a better chance to win the Australian Open".[29] Over and over again, Toni repeated to Rafa how big a day this was, how close he was to winning his first Australian Open title. A win here would almost certainly mean a changing of the guard, Rafa could cement his place at the top of the men's game, and Toni knew that. "Rafael, now, you are bad, very bad. But rest assured that in five hours, when you walk onto court, you won't be better. You will probably feel worse than now, when you see Federer on the other side of the net. Neither God or your father will come down and help you. You have to get through this moment by yourself. Nobody can do it for you".[29] It was a Toni Nadal special. Never had Rafa complained, and now wasn't the time to start. Rafa was, however, continuing to struggle in the practice session. He again made his feelings known to his coach. "I assure you that I can't move. My legs aren't responding to me. I can't run", he cried.[29] He should have known better than to complain, and to be expected, his complaints fell on deaf ears. "Nonsense! Sure you can run! If when you went on court, you were told that there was a sniper in the stands pointing a gun at you, saying he would shoot you when you stopped running, I assure you that you would not stop until you reached Mallorca. You can run, Rafael, you can run!"[29] Toni was in no way letting his nephew feel sorry for himself. Today of all days, there would be no excuses. All the harsh lessons and cruel to be kind methods of coaching were leading to this very moment. Toni always had a knack of saying things exactly how he saw them, and that morning was like no other.

To Toni's relief, a couple of hours before the final was due to start, he saw a shift in the attitude of Rafa. Rather than almost accepting defeat and falling victim to his own success in the semi-final, he began to listen to his coach. With the hours passing, Rafa finally started to release some of the tension. He started to show signs he was up for the fight. Evidence that he had not abandoned his confidence or his hope of winning were emerging.[29] A different coach may have put an arm around Rafa in those moments leading up to the final, but Toni was different. He still, after all these years, refused to let his nephew show anything but complete commitment and desire to win, no matter what the circumstances. Years of good habits, of fighting to give himself every possible chance were paying off. As the final began, the world looked on in anticipation.

The first set, whilst played with an abundance of grace and skill, was filled with tension. Despite finding himself 4-2 ahead and a break of serve up, Federer fell to a 5-7 defeat to give the Spaniard a one set to love lead. The second set went the way of the Swiss, with Rafa only managing to win three games. After another tie-break in the third set, Rafa managed to pull ahead, claiming the third set and going two sets to one ahead.

Tiredness then began to kick in for the Spaniard, as to be expected, and Federer picked up the fourth set comfortably, winning 6-3.

Somewhat surprisingly, considering the amount of hours Rafa had spent on court that tournament, it was Roger who first began to show signs of tiredness. Despite playing gloriously in the fourth set, he seemed to have hit a brick wall. The 3-time champion was showing signs of weakness, with his game becoming erratic and lackadaisical. Rafa, noticing his opponents struggles, seized the moment. In that final set, he found an inner strength. It was almost as though his uncle's words earlier that day were true, and there really was a sniper in the stands waiting to shoot him if he stopped running. He played as though his life depended on it. He chased down everything, finding energy when it appeared there was nothing left in the tank. There is no doubt Toni's words were heard loud and clear in his head. Every big point won or fantastic winner smashed past Federer, he would look to the players' box, with his fist clenched, making eye contact with his uncle.

"My nephew ended up overcoming all his pain and helplessness, and showed a strength that surprised us all, including me", confessed Toni.[29] After 4 hours and 23 minutes, Federer's forehand landed outside the court, and Rafa fell to the ground. He had won the Australian Open, when just hours earlier he could barely walk, let alone run. The endurance, resilience, will to win, and mental toughness had come together. Toni had created a well oiled mentality monster. Throughout the entirety of Rafa's career, not just that tournament in 2009, he has shown unrivaled attitude.

His coach taught him principles as a boy that he has taken with him throughout his professional career. His decision to stay with his uncle, when leaving for Barcelona would have been the ideal move on paper, shows the trust and belief Rafa placed in his coach. From sweeping the courts and picking up the balls after a session as an 8-year-old in Manacor, to becoming, at the time of writing this, a 20-time Grand Slam champion, Rafa never lost sight of what Toni taught him.

It's easier to think of great tennis coaches or leaders as people who create excellent morale within their camp, who control their tempers and possess exceptional emotional intelligence. That is perhaps the modern, and correct way, of summarising good leadership. Peter Carter and Tim Gullikson are perfect examples of that. Once in a while however, you get outliers. People like Steve Jobs, or Lyndon Johnson, the 36th President of the United States. If you look back throughout history, some of the world's leading figures have realised success through unconventional methods. A case in point can be seen with the man prior mentioned, Lyndon Johnson. People who worked under Johnson whilst he was a young and ambitious leader of the National Youth Association in 1935, claim working underneath him was at times extremely difficult. He wasn't afraid to yell, or lose his temper. If an employee had a cluttered desk, they were unorganised. If another member of staff had a clean and tidy desk, they weren't busy enough. Crucially, however, everybody knew they were part of a larger purpose. The belief each member of staff had in Johnson to get the job done was worth the difficulties that lay in working for him on a daily basis. Fast forward a number of decades, and you'll find similarities in Toni Nadal's style of coaching. As we have seen, there were times Rafa felt like arguing back with his coach, or giving up. But what the duo shared, just like the employees who worked for Johnson, was an overriding sense of common purpose. Without that, it's fair to assume that Toni's methods could have easily failed.[6]

When the duo amicably parted ways at the end of the 2017 season, Toni's life's work, and 25 years of coaching his nephew, had come to an end. From their first session to the last, Toni always made sure Rafa stuck to the principles that got them to were they are. They achieved 16 of Rafa's 20 Grand Slams together, and Toni's presence in Rafa's players' box around the world became a sight embedded in the sport of tennis.[33] Rafa's love of the game and incredible spirit has never been questioned. His respect for not only the sport but the people around him has always been a topic of discussion to coincide with his generational talent. When Toni looks back at what they achieved together, his nephew's character will no doubt be one of the accomplishments he is most proud of. As a player who never played top level tennis, his ability to train and groom his young nephew all the way to the top of the men's game is astounding.

He knew that it wasn't just Rafa that needed to continuously improve, but he had to consistently improve as a coach, too.

Table 3.1: Rafael Nadal Career Grand Slams by Year

2005	2006	2007	2008
French Open	French Open	French Open	French Open, Wimbledon
2009	**2010**	**2011**	**2012**
Australian Open	French Open, Wimbledon, U.S. Open	French Open	French Open
2013	**2014**	**2017**	**2018**
French Open, U.S. Open	French Open	French Open, U.S. Open	French Open
2019	**2020**		
French Open, U.S. Open	French Open		

Chapter Four

Marian Vajda & Novak Djokovic

"In my case, I can sincerely say nothing is impossible".

Novak Djokovic

WHEN TONI NADAL WALKED BY court number 18 in June 2005, he couldn't stop himself from watching the match taking place. Whilst Wimbledon is a Grand Slam steeped in history and tradition, you'll seldom find a top ranked player competing on one of the higher numbered courts. With his attention caught however, he took a seat, and focused his eyes on the match. On one side of the court was

Argentinian Juan Monaco, a close friend and hitting partner of Rafa's. On the other side, a Serbian player unknown to many.

Toni watched as the Serbian player outclassed Monaco, outplaying him in every aspect. This was no easy feat, Toni had seen Juan Monaco play countless times, he was in no way a pushover. To everybody's surprise, his low-ranked opponent was simply too good for him. He had a big serve, a dominant baseline game, and an abundant air of confidence that he exhibited with every shot. The match was wrapped up in no time at all, with Monaco falling victim to a straight sets defeat. Impressed, Toni checked the scoreboard to familiarise himself with the young Serbian's name and immediately headed towards the locker room, where Rafa was waiting. When he arrived, he shot over to his nephew.

"Rafael, we have a problem".
"How?", he replied.
"His name is Novak Djokovic, and he's playing Juan Monaco on court number 18".

2006 French Open

The French Open took place almost 12 months after Wimbledon, with the still relatively unknown Novak Djokovic drawn against Rafa Nadal in the quarter-finals.

A year younger than the Spaniard, Novak Djokovic was highly temperamental, but somebody who possessed immense talent. Aforementioned, the Serb was a player who was generating a buzz on the tour, and before their match, Rafa and Toni spoke in depth about how to beat him. The world number two was looking for back to back French Open titles, but had admitted to watching Novak in his rear-view mirror for a while, anticipating the day they met for the first time. It didn't take an experienced analyst of the game to see that before long, it would be Roger Federer, Rafa Nadal, and Novak Djokovic regularly competing for the top prizes in the sport. "Djokovic had a strong serve and was fast. He was powerful and often dazzling on both forehand and backhand. Above all, I could see he had big ambitions and a winner's attitude", said Rafa when analysing Novak's early game.[28]

Throughout their first match together in the quarter-final, Novak made it tough for his opponent. Rafa was at the beginning of his dominance on clay, and Novak, despite being more of a hard court player, gave him a tough afternoon. Not for the only time in Novak's early career however, he felt the need to retire from the match, citing breathing difficulties and back pain after losing the second set 6-4. The match was a tight affair, and everybody was disappointed to see Novak pull out and subsequently withdraw from the tournament. "I was serving at 40 or 50 per-cent maximum. I don't think it would have been good for me to continue playing. This is not the only tournament of the year", he confessed after the match.[34] Seeing Djokovic retire from a tournament was something of a regular occurrence. By 2010, he had retired 11 times from a number of events across the ATP Tour. Nevertheless, despite the defeat to Rafa Nadal at the French Open, his achievement of getting to the quarter-final meant he was now ranked in the top 50.

At the time of the 2006 French Open, Novak was playing without a full-time coach, which made his surge up the rankings even more remarkable. Riccardo Piatti, now the coach of teenage Italian prodigy Jannik Sinner, was the man responsible for coaching the young Serbian for the best part of a year until they parted ways before the start of Roland-Garros. Together, the Italian coach and Novak worked hard and spent a lot of time together, despite Piatti coaching other big names at the time. He has always spoken of his pride at seeing the success Djokovic has achieved, and often states that he knew Novak was destined for big things even at the ages of 17 and 18 when he was his coach. "When we worked together I thought he could become number one in the world at the level of Rafael Nadal and Roger Federer because Novak always worked hard as a kid, and he was very focused and determined to be world number one", he confessed.[35]

Despite the work the pair had put in together, which coincided with Novak's rise up the ATP rankings, the Serbian still hadn't made it past the third round of a Grand Slam, and there was a growing feeling he needed a coach who could dedicate themselves to him. To coincide with his task of coaching Novak Djokovic, who at the time had immense potential but wasn't a top ranked player, Piatti was also the coach of the Croatian Ivan Ljubicic. Ljubicic was at the peak of his career, and the pair had seen him rise to a career high of number three in the world in 2006. Whilst Piatti admitted that Novak would be a fantastic player to coach and work with full-time, his priority was very much the Croatian.[36] Novak was of course unhappy with the decision, and after careful consideration, he decided to part ways with the Italian. Piatti has always said that Novak is the best player he has ever worked with, and despite Djokovic's early disgruntlement at being snubbed by Piatti for Ljubicic, the split was entirely amicable, so much so that they are still close friends to this day.[36]

Djokovic's arrival into the world's top 50 further emphasised his need for a new coach who could not only work with him full-time, but help fulfil his life long ambition of being ranked the number one player in the world. Unlike Rafa, who had one man in his way if he was to become world number one, Novak had two. To conquer the world of tennis he not only had to overcome the king of grass in Roger Federer, but the most dominant player in clay court history in Rafa Nadal. He needed to choose his next coach wisely.

*

The Perfect Duo

In the lead up to the French Open, Djokovic was handed a list of coaches that could potentially take over from his former Italian tutor. On the list of names, was Slovakian Marian Vajda.

As a player, Vajda achieved a career high of number 34 in the ATP rankings in 1987. He belonged to a remarkable generation of tennis players from the former Czechoslovakia, who boasted 11 top 100 players throughout the 1980s. Like many other top players who go on to become excellent coaches, he was well known for his positive attitude and highly organised approach to the game. Similar to that of Toni Nadal and Peter Lundgren, his preference towards a more tactical playing style helped him achieve more in the game than his playing ability perhaps allowed. Vajda has described himself as being a combination of the following traits: organised, hardworking and disciplined.[37] The Czechoslovakian tennis system that Vajda had been brought up in had produced a number of stars, including Jan Kodes, Ivan Lendl and Martina Navratilova, all of whom went on to become Grand Slam champions. Being able to meet elite players as a junior had a greatly beneficial impact on not only the way he played the game, but the way he saw it, too. He witnessed first hand the dedication it takes to become a Grand Slam champion in the sport.[37]

Whilst playing on the tour, Vajda didn't have a coach that travelled with him. Travelling solo meant the Slovakian had to be extremely organised, as no coach meant planning his tennis career alone, deciding which steps to take next and which areas of improvement to work on. This certainly helped prepare Vajda for the coaching career that he would go on to pursue. He was intent on maximising his potential, and he was forced to learn how to do that quickly.[37] It is no secret that playing on the tour and coaching are two completely different jobs, but during his playing career he was as much his own coach as he was a player.

Post retirement, his first real venture into professional coaching came when he was appointed as the mentor of Dominik Hrbaty, a fellow Slovakian, whose most impressive career highlight was perhaps beating Roger Federer in Cincinnati in 2004. The time Vajda spent with Hrbaty was pivotal in his improvement as a coach. For the first time, he was tasked with squeezing the potential out of another player, rather than himself. To do this, he quickly understood and realised the importance of recognising a player's personality and social environment, with the aim of using that to fulfil potential on court.[37] After impressing as Hrbaty's coach, Vajda started working with Karol Kucera, a fellow compatriot and top ten player. This was the first time the Slovakian had an established top ten player on his hands, and thus presented a fresh batch of challenges. Coaching a player of Kucera's calibre meant a greater emphasis on the tactical and strategic side of the game. Kucera's career high of number six in the world meant Vajda could put his experience and tactical knowledge to the test against the world's best players on a regular basis.[37] The pair worked together from 2001-2005, a four year stint that saw Vajda's reputation grow as a fantastic man-manager with a leading tennis brain. By the end of the French Open in 2006, Novak Djokovic had been on the ATP Tour for two years, and felt as though the Slovakian was the right man to take over from Piatti. The appointment wasn't as easy as it seems however.

"Before Roland-Garros 2006, I was asked by an agency if I was interested in seeing Novak in Paris. I didn't know much about him, because he was only ranked 63rd before the tournament", said Vajda. At the time, he had been on the tour for a number of years as a player and a coach, and a break from the constant travelling had been at the forefront of his agenda. There was certainly a degree of hesitancy when he was first pitched with the idea of coaching Djokovic. After giving it some thought, he eventually decided to travel to France and watch Novak in an attempt to analyse his game.[38] Not only was the 2006 French Open a good opportunity for Vajda to witness Djokovic playing in action for the first time, it was also a chance to show his 11-year-old daughter the incredibly beautiful city of Paris, so he decided to take her along with him. Whilst deciding whether or not to become Novak's new coach, it was in fact his daughter, a keen tennis player herself, who convinced him.[36] An agreement was made, and for Novak's subsequent tournament in Hertogenbosch, Holland, he would have Marian Vajda in his players' box.

Within a matter of weeks, Djokovic's immense talent and outrageous potential had massively impressed his new coach, and Vajda was primed for the challenges that lay ahead.[36] The duo immediately saw eye to eye, largely due to the core values they shared. Just like his coach, discipline and professionalism made up the foundations of Novak's tennis life. He figured out extremely early that if he wanted to reach the top of the sport, there could be no victim mentality or weak inner mind. Coming from Serbia, a country whose citizens often talk about how unfairly the country has been treated, Djokovic knew that his mentality had to be different than what is the norm in his native country.[36]

The first coach to ever give the Serb tennis lessons at the age of 6, Jelena Gencic, has often spoke about the time she spent with a young Novak. There are endless tales of Jelena giving advice to her student, but the way in which Djokovic responded was far different to the other boys his age. He would show intelligence of somebody much his elder. Despite understanding exactly what was asked of him, he always wanted further clarification so that he could master the task he'd been handed. Whenever his coach would ask him if he understood what she had said, he would reply "yes, but please tell me again". He wanted to understand completely what he was being asked, in a bid to maximise his improvement.[39] There are other stories of Novak arranging to play with somebody at a certain time, only to actually get out on court and start hitting shots way before they arrived. This most notably happened with former Croatian player Nikki Pilic, who had agreed to hit with the young Serbian, and upon arriving, saw Djokovic already out playing. He was just a number of people impressed with Djokovic's work ethic at such a young age. Australian born Serbian tennis coach Dejan Petrovic was also taken aback by the drive Djokovic had upon seeing him for the first time. Before every practice session he would arrive 15 or 20 minutes early to stretch and jog around the court. "He was a perfectionist in every way", claimed Petrovic. "I saw that he wasn't 'from Serbia' – if he'd been a typical Serbian, he'd have come on time, or maybe even a few minutes late. You could see that he was from somewhere else".[36] It appeared Djokovic was born with a burning desire to be the best, and knew the only way to get there was by being the ultimate professional. It was a trait that worked hand in hand with the principles of Vajda, his new coach. Already, it was a match made in heaven.

Becoming The Best

Although Vajda knew he was working with a great talent, there were flaws to Novak's game that needed addressing, and they needed addressing urgently. As previously mentioned, witnessing Djokovic retire from a match wasn't unusual. In fact, just a few years into his life as a professional tennis player, he had gained a rather unwelcome reputation of being a quitter. In regards to Grand Slams, by 2009, Novak had surrendered on multiple occasions. He retired mid-match at the French Open in 2005 against Guillermo Coria, in his quarter-final match against Rafa Nadal at the French Open in 2006, his semi-final match against the Spaniard at Wimbledon the following year, and then again against Andy Roddick in the quarter-final of the Australian Open in 2009. He was dipping out of matches at a rate far greater than that of other players on the tour. For example, at the time of writing this, Roger Federer has played in 1,511 matches. He has completed every single one of them.[40] Despite this being an incredible statistic, and one perhaps unfairly used to compare with Djokovic's record, it does highlight the alarming rate in which Novak was feeling the need to retire mid-match, and subsequently hand his opponent victory. If you compare that Novak Djokovic to the man we see on court today, he is a different animal. He is leaner, fitter, and his rate of withdrawing from tournaments mid-way through matches has decreased emphatically. There is no doubt that Marian Vajda has played a pivotal role in this sharp upturn in success.

After his retirement from the Australian Open in 2009, Vajda and Novak both knew something had to be done in regards to his failure to complete matches. Just two years later in 2011, his year was ranked as the third greatest tennis season in the open era by Tennis Magazine. Throughout 2011, he won Wimbledon, the Australian Open, and the U.S. Open, and won a staggering 70 matches across all tournaments. Rafa Nadal faced Novak in two of his three Grand Slam finals, and later said that the level of tennis Novak played that year was "probably the highest level of tennis that I ever saw".[41] A profound statement that indicates the level Djokovic and Vajda had reached. He had found a doggedness and resoluteness that was lacking beforehand. But how did this happen?

For a while, Novak was sat behind Roger Federer and Rafael Nadal in the rankings. There are certainly worse places to rank than number three in the world, and for Novak, it was relatively easy to stay there. He had worked incredibly hard as a junior and as a result he had risen rapidly up the world rankings as a professional. His game was tidy and efficient, he defended impeccably, and there wasn't really an urgent need to drastically improve any other parts of his game. Perhaps, when he found himself as the third best player in the world, he saw it as an opportunity to coast. Monetary gain was no real motivation, he had earned millions in prize money already, so the question came down to how hard he wanted to work to take the final and most difficult step in his career. It's obvious that the Serb put his heart and soul into every match, but that is the easy part. To overtake Rafa and Roger, he needed to put everything he had into the mental and physical side of the game, too. The parts that the crowds and TV cameras don't see. Djokovic had always been equipped with tremendous levels of discipline, but there is no doubt that he sat down with

Marian Vajda around the year 2009 and ultimately decided that he wasn't satisfied with being the world number three. Motivation, amongst other factors, including drive, passion and desire, is one of the game's primary psychological skills.[11] Research has found that motivation is one of the hardest mental skills for coaches to teach when working with top junior players, however.[42] Despite not being an issue for Djokovic whilst playing as a junior, it could be argued that for a brief period, the Serb's motivational climate was ego-orientated. Rather than reinforcing the importance of his progress, he would spend more time worried about the outcome of his matches. Whilst winning the majority of his duels, he would ultimately fall short when competing against Rafa and Roger, which may have led to a lack of motivation. He had to work harder, and realise his losses should not be punished, but accepted as part of a learning process. He knew he had the right coach to shift his mentality and improve his performance, so they got to work on taking over the world of men's tennis.

The first change the pair implemented came off the court. Whilst a lot has been said about Novak Djokovic's change of diet in 2010, it's clear that his switch to a gluten-free style of eating did have a positive impact. Those involved in professional sport will be familiar with the term 'the one percenters' - the aim of looking for any advantage to gain a slight edge. As far as Djokovic and Vajda were concerned when identifying ways to progress, the Serb's diet certainly belonged in the one per-cent

category.   Together, the pair worked closely with doctor
Igor Cetojevic.   Cetojevic did a number of tests on Djokovic,
and found that he was intolerant to certain foods that he
regularly ate, including gluten, dairy products and tomatoes.[43]
Tennis players are regularly exposed to high intensity training,
prolonged matches, and heavy travel schedules - none more
so perhaps than Novak himself.   Players have reported to
have travelled more than 48,000 miles in a two-month period
whilst on the tour, with international and domestic flights the
most common way to travel.[11] To combat the performance
decrements that coincide with constant travelling, efficient
nutritional practices are incredibly important to aid recovery
and improve performance. Eating foods likely to have a detrimental effect on the Serb was a huge problem. Immediately, a
new diet was put into place, with refined sugar removed and
nutrient-dense carbohydrates added. Carbohydrates provide
a vital food source to all athletes, sending energy via the
aerobic and anaerobic pathways, meaning Djokovic felt better
mentally as well as physically.[11] Despite losing some weight
early in the process, Novak quickly put the pounds back on,
and subsequently found he could breathe much easier on court,
leading to greater energy levels and faster recovery in between
training and matches.[43]

Whilst improvements were made to Novak's food intake, it
should be mentioned that his almost superhero like transformation from a "quitter" to the best player in the sport cannot
be pinpointed to one simple change. Even before the overhaul

of his diet, Novak was a Grand Slam winner under the tutelage of Vajda, and could still compete in matches that lasted for hours on end. It would therefore be naive to say that a lack of gluten in Novak's diet was the sole reason for his sudden success, although it certainly did help. The change in eating habits coincided with hard, regular practice and technical tweaks to the Serbian's on court game. Developments were being made in all aspects of Djokovic's tennis life, much to the credit of his coach. In a way similar to Abraham Lincoln creating a "team of rivals" after becoming President of the United States, Vajda also decided to add more input into Novak's team.

Former U.S. President Abraham Lincoln's election win in 1861 was great testimony to his genius as a politician. Most people in power, whether that be in business, politics, or sport, surround themselves with like-minded company who agree with them on nearly all aspects. Whilst having a long list of positives, surrounding yourself with people who blindly support your opinion does have its fair share of downfalls. Upon winning the election, Lincoln assembled the most unusual cabinet in American history. The former President's success was tied to his decision to create a team of independent, strong minded individuals, all of whom shared different political ideas to that of himself. The best leaders have the confidence to surround themselves with people who may question their authority in a bid to create diverse opinions. When Marian Vajda added Todd Martin to the team, he did just that. Whilst Martin was never going to outwardly question the authority of Vajda, he was a respected coach with his own ideas, and brushing shoulders with somebody who may have disagreed with his views on Novak's training could have become problematic. Vajda showed tremendous strength of character by incorporating another coach into the vicinity. Similar to other great coaches and leaders, he accepted a flaw in his coaching ability, and sought out help to combat it. Humility is often described as humbleness, but what it really is, is an awareness of your limitations so that you can learn from them.[6]

The area of improvement that Vajda was looking to develop was Novak's serve. Around mid 2009, Andy Murray had burst onto the scene, and the Scotsman was threatening to take over from Novak as the world number three. The Serb had his eyes on becoming number one, so falling down a place to number four didn't sit well with him. His serve needed improvement, and Todd Martin was brought in to help with that. The decision was an interesting choice. The American wasn't a particularly magnificent player, although he did reach the final rounds of a couple of Grand Slams in his playing career. Overall, however, he was a very likable man, and the duo of Djokovic and Vajda saw him as the ideal candidate to help progress the Serbian's game. "They felt they needed someone with a stronger playing background, with experience in the latter stages of Grand Slams", recalled Martin.[36] At a tournament in Dubai in 2010, Djokovic's serve was his biggest defect. His technique wasn't right, according to Martin. "The most important issue needing to be resolved was the fact that his elbow stayed straight until the very last second of the forward and upward swing, so it was never consistently loaded".[36] In the tournament in Dubai, Djokovic constantly hit double faults and his serve was broken in almost every set of the tournament - yet amazingly he still won. That emphasised his mental strength and the improvements he was making to the other aspects of his game. Whilst Martin was only part of the team for a few months, he did highlight some key areas of improvements that could help transform Novak's serve, and Vajda has often been vocal of his thanks to Martin.[36]

It may have only been a subtle change, but Vajda went against the norm in that situation. He brought somebody in who had different ideas on how Novak should serve. Ideas that went against what the duo were working on at the time. Djokovic's serve was subsequently changed and improved, and there were many other occasions where Vajda looked to bring people into the team who had their own opinions on his player - Boris Becker's arrival into the Djokovic camp in 2013 is another example of that. The array of diverse opinions created a better Novak Djokovic.

*

Practice Makes Perfect

"Tennis cannot be based on a philosophy", claims Vajda. "It's a hand to hand sport. If you want to be at the top, the path is through practice and repetition, and a good mentality".[36] Vajda is a keen advocate of hard on court training. In a way dissimilar to Toni Nadal, he emphasises his on court work with Novak more than the mental side, although that's not to say he completely disregards the psychological side of the game. When it came to defeating Rafael Nadal, however, most of the work had to be done during practice sessions.

For a number of years, Nadal had completely blown Novak away whenever they met at the French Open. This was no embarrassment, as many of the top pros, including Roger Federer, struggled to get a single set against him in the French capital, let alone win a match. Despite winning every other Grand Slam on more than one occasion, the Spaniard's dominance on clay had proved a titanic hurdle for Novak Djokovic in his quest to be regarded as the greatest player of all time. Up until 2016, the French Open was the only Grand Slam missing from his magnificent array of trophies.

Surprisingly, Marian Vajda claims Novak's favourite surface was in fact clay when he first turned professional.[44] This is a common theme amongst top junior players who make the transition into the men's game. For example, seven out of the ten boys who won the U.S. Open Junior Championships between 1990-2000, all grew up playing on clay. It's therefore no surprise that when the pair originally started working together, a lot of their early tournament wins actually came on clay. It may appear that Novak adapted his game to suit that specific surface, but it was actually the other way around. He worked hard to shift his style to become a brilliant grass and hard court player.[44] By the time Rafa had defeated Djokovic for the sixth time at Roland-Garros however, both Vajda and Novak felt enough was enough. Going into the 2015 season, the duo put all their focus and attention on beating Rafa in Paris. They were determined to add the only Grand Slam missing to their collection of trophies, and knew hard on court work was the only way to do it.

"As a coach, I had to look for improvement in his game on clay. He had to adapt his game because Rafael is a very strong and powerful player",[44] confessed Vajda. As previously mentioned in the last chapter, clay is a surface that suits the Spaniard's style perfectly. The heavy top spin he uses is effective in slowing the game down, and Djokovic, along with countless other players, have often struggled to generate enough speed when returning his shots. Vajda knew that his client had to improve his strength and power if he was to come out victorious.[45] Showing the ability that made him one of the world's leading coaches, he identified certain ways he could help Novak overcome his Iberian nemesis. The key areas that Vajda began to work on with Djokovic were as follows:

*

I. Despite having an athletic build perfect for tennis, the Slovak thought it necessary to strengthen his muscles. To achieve this, his coach made slight changes to Djokovic's diet. "His diet is dominantly vegetarian, but he needed some animal proteins as well. It's not possible without those. That is why Novak has adjusted his diet to include eating more fish as he doesn't eat other kinds of meat", declared Vajda.[45] After adding a careful amount of animal foods to Novak's daily eating habits, his coach felt his muscles were in better condition, giving him added strength which he could use to great effect against Rafa. This was a heavily thought out decision, as the general consensus was that meat had been partly to blame for some of Novak's prior on court breathing difficulties. What they didn't want to do was give birth to more mid-match retirements.

II. In regards to on court changes, there were a couple of improvements deemed vital if they were to breach the Rafa Nadal bastion in Paris. Firstly, in the 2014 French Open final between Djokovic and Nadal, Vajda felt as though he was out-hit by his opponent. Despite winning the first set, Nadal stormed his way to victory, winning the following three sets comfortably to win the tournament for the ninth time. To combat this, the pair worked on taking the ball much earlier, thus speeding the game up and giving his opponent less time to prepare.[44] The duo would spend hours on the practice court, working on taking the ball on the rise, rather than letting the ball bounce high, which makes it harder to generate any real power to cause serious problems. This, in turn, would minimise the time Rafa had to not only get to the ball, but to produce one of his magnificent top spin shots. As well as enabling Novak to play quicker tennis, it would help to neutralise Rafa's strengths simultaneously.

III. Surprisingly, the final improvement involved Novak's backhand. Djokovic is often credited as having the best backhand in the sport. It's a truly formidable shot, and has been for the majority of his career. On clay however, against Rafa, it didn't suffice. "He had to improve his backhand and shut down the point. He had to be aggressive and dominate the game", explained Vajda.[44] Flattening out the Serbian's backhand to make it more attacking became the main focus in practice sessions throughout 2015. Taking the ball on the rise, as well as hitting a flatter, harder and faster backhand was the key to success according to Djokovic's coach.

To coincide with the specific areas of improvement that Vajda identified in regards to overcoming Rafa, Djokovic also started to hit his forehand a lot harder during that time, according to his coach. Strength training had been consistent in Novak's training since Vajda arrived, and it was slowly starting to pay off.[36] Unlike other field or court sports, a tennis player isn't tasked with using their power to directly out muscle an opponent. Instead, an increase in strength is used to generate racquet velocity and to increase the speed in which a player can change direction.[11] Tennis players can change direction as many as fifteen times per point, and research has shown a direct correlation between a player's strength and their ability to move around the court at an increased speed.[46] Vajda, along with fitness coach Gebhard Phil-Gritsch, helped to majorly develop this aspect of the Serb's game. Djokovic has described the trio as a "team with a capital T".[47]

Many of the training methods that Vajda implemented during this time, he still uses today.   With emphasis on resistance training, Djokovic ensures that there is a focus on muscle group specificity, making sure his core is strong which in turn creates better balance. Marian Vajda deserves immense credit for the refinements he made to Novak's daily routines, with the above methods leading to an increase in balance, speed at which he could change direction, and power in his ground strokes. The Serb's added strength also improved his linear and rotational movements in his torso and arms, which subsequently resulted in a much harder forehand.[11]

For any tennis player to hit a great shot, it is commonly accepted that having a stable base is a must. As we have seen, players change direction countless times throughout a point, so the ability to decelerate is just as important as accelerating. Off the mark speed must be met with rapid deceleration to ensure a player is stable and balanced before making contact with the ball.[11] Marian Vajda and Novak Djokovic worked tirelessly on improving the strength in Novak's frontal plane e.g. lunging from side to side to hit strokes. As Roland-Garros' surface requires players to hit shots whilst 'skating' as Rafa calls it,[28] the added work on this area proved crucial to the Serb's clay court game. He could now use his added strength to hit shots whilst sliding and lunging for the ball.

Although it took time and patience, by the time the 2015 French Open came around, Novak Djokovic, along with his trusted coach and mentor Marian Vajda, felt ready to end the agonising succession of defeats against Rafa at the French Open.

Overcoming Rafa

There was something different in the air when the first round of matches began to unfold at the French Open on the 24th of May, 2015. A quick glance at the ATP world rankings would emphasise that. At the top of the list, was Novak Djokovic. After his record breaking year in 2011, it was evident that the world number one had upped his game to yet another level. After years of fighting to step out of the gargantuan shadow that Roger Federer and Rafa Nadal had created, he had earned the right to have his name spoken alongside them when debating the greatest player of all time. He was now seated at the table of tennis's elite, and it was just where Marian Vajda had envisaged he would end up when he started working with the Serbian.

On the contrary, Rafa Nadal was in the midst of one his most difficult patches of form. His usual air of invincibility on clay had begun to show signs of vulnerability. In the lead up to Roland-Garros, the Spaniard had suffered defeats to Fabio Fognini in both Rio and Barcelona, Andy Murray in Madrid, and Stan Wawrinka in Rome. His form had dipped, along with his standing in the world rankings. When he began his first round match of the French Open against wildcard Quentin Halys, he was sixth, and that subsequently created problems. It meant drawing Novak Djokovic in the quarter-final if the pair both reached that stage of the competition.

Both Djokovic and Nadal raced through their opening matches, with Novak's most notable win coming against former world number seven, Richard Gasquet. The Frenchman was powerless to resist the added elements of Djokovic's clay court game. Marian Vajda looked on from the players' box as he watched his client complete another straight set's victory, defeating Gasquet 6-1, 6-2, 6-3, to set up that mouth watering quarter-final with Nadal.

Perhaps it was a blessing and a curse that the pair met so early in the tournament. It meant Djokovic had spent considerably less time on court than he usually would have done before stepping out to play Rafa at a Grand Slam. In that sense, he was fresher. He had won all his matches in straight sets so far in the tournament, so tiredness wasn't going to be an issue. One downside, however, was that the immense mental and physical effort it was going to take to beat Rafa meant if he did progress to the next round, he would have to recover quickly, and immediately face another world class opponent in the semi-final. Either way, the stage was set, and the moment Novak and his coach had been waiting for all season had arrived. This was his chance to stop the Spaniard on his favoured surface. Six times the pair had met at the French open, and each time it had resulted in a win for Nadal.

Djokovic came out aggressively, taking his shots early, and firing his backhand much flatter than the year previous, much to the delight of his coach. Within twenty minutes, the first set read 4-0 to the Serb. With Djokovic forced way beyond the baseline, Rafa's forehand drop shot agonisingly struck the top of the net, giving Novak his second break of serve. The French crowd roared, and a disgruntled Rafa looked up towards his uncle for some encouragement. Whether it was a lapse in concentration, or early signs of nervousness, Djokovic immediately let Rafa back into the set, over-hitting his forehand by a couple of yards on break point to allow Rafa his first game of the match. Before long, it was 4-4. Despite playing well and using the new instructions taught by Vajda, Rafa's sheer clay court excellence had levelled the first set. Much to his credit, Djokovic didn't show any signs of being perturbed by his opponents comeback, and remained diligent to the game plan set out by his coach. After an hour of back and forth action, Djokovic had finally landed himself a set point. Rafa's thunderous serve was sent wide to his backhand. Using all the practice he had endured, he met the ball early, hit a flat and hard backhand down the line to Rafa, who could only manage a weak shot to the forehand of Djokovic. Using his added strength, he bolted to the opposite side of the court, decelerated, lunged, stayed perfectly balanced, and hit a hard forehand cross-court, leaving Rafa with no option but to stretch and volley the ball wide. A fantastic shot, and one that may not have been possible a year earlier. As Nadal's shot landed out, Djokovic looked to Vajda, simultaneously pumping his fist. It was the best hour of tennis he had ever played against Rafa at the French Open, and there was more of the same to come.[44]

In the following 18 games, Djokovic won 14 of them. His added power, core strength, and technical efficiency was proving far too difficult for Rafa to overcome. With each major point won, the Serb couldn't help but glance towards his coach. After taking the second set 6-3, the world number one was on course to dispose of his rival in an enthralling manner. Any hopes of a Rafael Nadal comeback vanished in the opening game of the third set. When the Spaniard's smash fell right to Djokovic, the Serb took the ball on the rise, and fired the ball right back at Rafa, who, not for the first time, volleyed wide. The French crowd were witnessing a masterclass from the Serb. Nobody had seen Nadal so emphatically outclassed at Roland-Garros before, but then again, they hadn't witnessed the year of hard work Novak had put in for this moment with his coach. The decision to turn Djokovic's already brilliant backhand into a flatter, more attacking shot was significantly neutralising Rafa's strengths. By the final game of the match, the result was already a foregone conclusion. When Nadal double faulted at match point, Djokovic wasn't overcome with emotion as you might expect. He'd known for a while he was going to win, and so had everybody watching. Everything he and his coach had worked on had been perfect in stopping Rafa claiming his 10th French Open title, at least for another year. This was Nadal's tournament, it was very much his turf. To beat him so comfortably, although it looked straightforward on paper, took its toll on Djokovic, according to his coach.

"I remember that it was a big relief to beat Rafael", recalls Vajda. "Maybe the joy of that win took off a lot of concentration for the final".[44] Vajda felt as though Novak's exertions from playing Nadal left him mentally fatigued. After all, he had just become the first man to beat Nadal in straight sets at the French Open, his achievement was unprecedented. The match against the Spaniard felt more like a final than a quarter-final, and the events that followed certainly showed evidence of that.

Less than 48 hours after dethroning Rafa, Andy Murray was the next man in line to face Djokovic. If the quarter-final match wore Novak down mentally, his semi-final match proved extremely physically demanding. Defeating Britain's

Andy Murray would mean a 28th consecutive victory across all competitions, but it was going to take a humongous effort to add another victory to his list. The match ended in a five set thriller. 6-3, 6-3, 5-7, 5-7, 6-1. The match swung one way, and then another. It was the Serbian's ruthlessness in crucial moments that helped him prevail, and it was a trait that tennis fans became accustomed to from Djokovic from 2010 onwards. Murray had been on a fifteen game unbeaten run on clay going into the match, but could do nothing to stop an eighth successive defeat at the hands of Djokovic. Again, using the skill set he now possessed after hours of training with Vajda, he had become a dominant clay court player. After earning his right to play in the final, where he would face Stan Wawrinka, he was one game away from completing a career Grand Slam. In 2015 however, it proved one step too far.

Competitive tennis requires a player to overcome two significant mental challenges. One is concerned with the opponent, and the other is internal - fighting their inner demons.[11] It's true that a player's mental state whilst competing in a match will undoubtedly affect the physical aspects of their game. Mental skills aren't inherent to players, however, and Vajda worked hard with Novak on his psychological framework. It wasn't just the change in diet or relentless on court training, Vajda helped Djokovic in his quest to nullify his trend of retiring mid-match for one reason or another. He had instilled a tougher, champion like mentality. For any psychological change to come to fruition, both player and coach have to work in harmony, and it's clear that both Novak and Vadja did that. In that French Open Final against Wawrinka however, the magnitude of his achievements seemed to get the better of him. "Stan deserved that win because Novak felt the pressure of beating Rafael and Andy, and being a big favourite in the final", declared Vajda. Djokovic was an overwhelming favourite to beat his Swiss opponent, having beaten Wawrinka 17 out of the 20 times they had played one another. Whilst being expected to win a Grand Slam final wasn't necessarily new to Djokovic, he had never been expected to win at the French Open, and according to his coach, it seemed to break the Serbian's mental strength. Throughout the final, Djokovic was outplayed. Wawrinka's 59 winning shots completely outweighed that of his opponent, who managed only 30. The defeat was Novak's third in a French Open Final, and despite achieving his goal of defeating Rafa, he had fallen short at the last hurdle. Fortunately, he wouldn't have to wait much longer to claim his first Roland-Garros title.

A Champion In Paris

As the years passed, winning the French Open became a dream for Novak Djokovic.[48] After an extremely disappointing defeat in the final a year prior to Wawrinka, many people thought success in France wasn't destined for the Serbian world number one. In his coach, however, he had a mentor who knew he could conquer his demons and emerge victorious. Whilst speaking on the Tennis Podcast, Marian Vajda admitted that Djokovic was overwhelmed with nerves going into the tournament in 2016. "Roland Garros is the most difficult and toughest tournament to win. You need to play seven best-of-five set matches on clay", he confessed.[48] Losing in three finals is enough to shake anybody's confidence, and going into his fourth final, where he would face Andy Murray, he was a bundle of anxiety. "He was really really nervous. He was all over the place. There was incredible tension", claimed Vajda.[48] It is moments like those where coaches can prove their worth. Vajda knew matches on clay have the potential to go on for extended periods of time, and instructed Djokovic not to panic if he lost the opening couple of sets. Novak had far greater stamina than his opponent, and his coach began to prepare him for the eventuality that the match could go on for a number of hours. As part of the game plan, he told Novak to use more spin if he was losing control of the match, that way, points would last longer and Novak's stamina could prove vital. The way Vajda saw it, the longer the match went on, the better chances they had of winning the French Open for the first time.[48]

Andy Murray was playing perhaps the best tennis of his career around 2016, and was certainly reaching new levels on clay. It presented a greater challenge than the final a year before. He knew it wasn't going to be easy, but with the right game plan, Djokovic's Slovakian coach felt confident.

*

It took just under an hour for the first set to reach its climax. Djokovic's nerves seemed to get the better of him, and with an uncharacteristic unforced error off his backhand, Murray took the first set. Whilst Murray jumped for joy and raced towards his seat, Djokovic strolled back, shrugging his shoulders in disgust at his first set performance. It was here that Vajda's words of advice before the match were imperative. Aforementioned, finding the value of a coach is often difficult, but in the French Open final in 2016, Marian Vajda proved just how important coaches are to tennis players. As soon as the second set began, Novak switched his playing style. "Novak started to impart more spin on the ball. He was more patient. In the second set, he felt he could win the match", confessed Vajda. By adding more spin to his shots, he began to wear his opponent down. Andy Murray couldn't find his rhythm, and succumbed to Djokovic 6-1. Using the advice of Vajda, he had discovered the blueprint to beat Murray on clay. Dropping only six games across the final two sets, he was relentless in his mission to bury his past failures in Paris. The final result ended 3-6, 6-1, 6-2, 6-4. As he fell to the ground, Vajda jumped out of his seat. The career Grand Slam that the duo had worked so hard for had finally happened. It had taken ten years, but Vajda had taken Novak from a young and talented player, looking up at the world's best, to a career Grand Slam winner and outright best player in the world. "There were celebrations that night in Paris. We went out and celebrated as a team together. We had a nice dinner and enjoyed the evening. It will stay in the memory forever, as

Novak accomplished something big", Vajda recalled.[48]

It may only have been a subtle change, but instructing Djokovic to add more spin to his shots was the catalyst that sparked Novak into life. The Serb had a coach who knew him inside and out, who had constructed his game to the point where multiple game plans could be given to his student to use in a match. If plan A wasn't working, Vajda had a plan B, and a plan C for that matter. Djokovic, around 2010, began to find ways to beat opponents under any circumstance. Playing styles make tennis matches, and Djokovic has the ability to change his style to consistently emerge victorious. His record breaking seasons and history of consecutive wins are testament to that. His coach deserves an immense amount of credit for the outright dominance Novak has claimed over the game of men's tennis for the best part of a decade.

ATP Coach of the Year

The list of reasons Marian Vajda became the ATP Coach of the Year in 2018 is an extraordinarily long one. Amongst the other candidates to take the crown that year, were Jan de Witt - coach of Nikoloz Basilashvili, Carlos Moya - the man chosen to take over from Toni Nadal to become Rafa's coach, Sebastian Prieto - coach of Juan Martin Del Potro, and Simone Vagnozzi - coach of Marco Cecchinato. It was a strong year in regards to coaching, with any of the coaches just mentioned deserving of the award. The events of the previous year however, added further strings to Vajda's already illustrious bow, and left him as a front runner for the accolade.

The ATP Coach of the Year award is perhaps the most prestigious individual prize a tennis coach can win. Voted for by fellow coaches on the ATP Tour, the award is given to the coach who helped guide their player, or players, to greater levels of performance throughout that specific year. In 2018, nobody did that better than the Slovakian.

A year prior, Novak Djokovic decided to part ways with both Vajda and fitness coach Gebhard Phil-Gritsch. The decision caused shock waves throughout the sport. The success Djokovic had achieved with Vajda had been unprecedented, but even the incredible array of Grand Slam victories didn't stop the Serb from making his decision. "I am forever grateful to Marian for a decade of friendship, professionalism and commitment to my career goals. Without his support I couldn't have achieved these professional heights", claimed Novak when speaking of their split.[49]

Whilst Djokovic had gone through a patchy spell of form, having lost his world number one spot to Andy Murray a few months beforehand, his decision was still met with scepticism. It did seem on the outside like a knee-jerk reaction. It was the first real dip in form since the duo began their professional relationship together, and Novak's slip down the rankings may have caused a sense of panic. Nevertheless, the decision was made, and Novak set off for the Madrid Open in 2017 without a coach.

By June the following year, Novak had fallen to number 22 in the ATP world rankings. It was a huge fall from grace when you consider his relative dominance of the previous seven years. It should be mentioned that losing matches at a rate greater than before wasn't the only factor in Djokovic's dip in the standings. After crashing out of the Australian Open in 2018 to South Korean Chung Hyeon, Novak underwent an operation on his right elbow which subsequently ruined the first half of his season. The straight sets loss to Hyeon in the fourth round was a huge shock however, and Hyeon himself couldn't quite believe it. "I didn't know how I'd win this tonight", he confessed after defeating Novak after three hours of action.[50] Injured or not, it was clear Novak Djokovic wasn't the same player without his coach. He was now a man accustomed to going deep into Grand Slam tournaments, and the fourth round loss created a need to evaluate his coaching situation.

Three months after his crushing loss in January at the Australian Open, Djokovic reunited with Vajda. The decision made perfect sense, as Novak never really looked the same after the pair parted ways. He was struggling in a number of ways. The Serbian's confidence was low, his form poor, and what he needed was a familiar voice to find his winning spark again. After receiving the call from Novak at his home in Bratislava, Slovakia, Vajda, like he had done in the past, asked for the opinion of his family. The answer was clear. "Frankly, they all said that they have a desire to see Novak back at the top again", said a buoyant Vajda who couldn't help but smile. "He called me and we talked almost one hour. I caught him full of doubts and he asked me about my opinion on his tennis. He wasn't clear on how his game should look". Vajda had also received offers to coach other players after he had stopped working with Novak, but found it difficult to see himself working with anybody but the Serb.[45]

Earlier in the season, Novak had crashed out of the BNP Paribas Open and the Miami Open in the first round. It wasn't going to be easy, but when the decision was made to join forces again, everybody involved felt ready to shake Djokovic free of his tennis abyss and see him rise back to the top of the rankings.

It had been less than a year since the split, but Vajda had already seen flaws in the Serbian's game that he looked to improve instantly. Due to his elbow injury, Djokovic had slightly changed the motion of his serve, designed to reduce the stress to his elbow. Even several months after his operation, Novak's serve wasn't the same as it was before. The racquet head was still moderately lower than it had been, and as a result created issues.[51]

Vajda, upon studying Novak's serve, wasn't overly impressed with what he saw. "His motion, there was a lot of good things but also some things I didn't like biomechanically", he confessed. When the pair began preparations for the 2018

French Open, under Vajda's guidance, Novak altered his service motion once more, allowing him to hit kick serves far more effectively.[51] This last change was a major factor in Djokovic's ability to get to the quarter-final of Roland Garros. Even just a couple of years prior, a quarter-final defeat would have felt like a disappointment in the Djokovic camp, but not this time around. Novak's run in the French Open that year was a sense of relief and cause for renewed optimism.[51] He was back playing high level tennis again. Djokovic was excited for the future with his coach back by his side, and at Wimbledon, he finally got back to his best.

At the start of the 2018 season, Djokovic had been eliminated from the Australian Open by a relatively unknown player, faced time out of the tour through injury, and suffered a number of first round losses. By the end of the year, he had won Wimbledon, the U.S. Open, and had climbed his way back to the top spot in the rankings. The man most responsible for such an upturn in form, outside of Novak himself, was of course Marian Vajda. He had once again proved the unrivalled value of a tennis coach. A position that is so often underappreciated.

Of course, upon receiving his award at the end of the year for best coach, he expressed happiness, not at winning an accolade for himself, but joy that his player had claimed the world number one spot once again. "I am really glad that after coming back, he reached number one in the world", he confessed whilst accepting his award at the ceremony.[52] Perhaps that is one of Vajda's most impressive attributes, his tunnel vision - his relentless quest to see Novak become the best player of all time, a desire that burned inside both player and coach. Nobody was surprised when Vajda won the ATP Coach of the Year in 2018.

In Novak Djokovic and Marian Vajda, you have the most successful player/coach combination in the history of the sport. It is rare for a player to stick with one coach for the majority of their career, but it's a decision that Djokovic will be forever grateful for. At the time of writing this, the duo have won 17 Grand Slam titles together, and you'd be a brave individual to bet against them winning another.

Table 4.1: Novak Djokovic Career Grand Slams by Year

2008	2011	2012	2013	2014
Australian Open	Australian Open Wimbledon U.S. Open	Australian Open	Australian Open	Wimbledon

2015	2016	2018	2019	2020
Australian Open Wimbledon U.S. Open	Australian Open French Open	U.S. Open Wimbledon	Australian Open Wimbledon	Australian Open

Chapter Five

Serena Williams

*"I really think a champion is defined not by their
wins but by how they can recover when they fall".*

Serena Williams

W̲HEN RICHARD WILLIAMS asked Rick Macci to travel to
Compton, California to assess his daughters' tennis
ability, his initial thoughts weren't as you might expect.

As a respected tennis coach, best known for guiding a young
Jennifer Capriati to international stardom, Macci hadn't heard
much in regards to the two American sisters. After a telephone
call with the girls' father, however, he made the decision to fly
out and watch them train. This was unusual, as most junior
tennis players are known throughout the circuit. They all play

in the same tournaments and it means coaches can get a good look at a lot of the best young stars. The same can't be said for the Williams sisters. They were essentially kept a secret. They didn't enter many tournaments at the request of their father, and the hype surrounding them was very much word of mouth. It was more a feeling of curiosity than excitement when Macci flew out to watch them train in the early 1990s.

Upon his arrival at the East Compton Hills Country Club, Venus and Serena began practicing. They hit balls back and forth to one another, fired a few serves, and trained some volleys. After a short while, Macci stepped in and set out some drills for the two girls to work on, in a bid to further analyse their game and overall tennis acumen. You could be forgiven for thinking he was probably completely blown away at that moment, the first time he laid eyes on the future multiple Grand Slam winners. But in truth, he wasn't. The American coach had seen a number of top young players throughout his coaching career, and had a keen eye for spotting potential. In Venus and Serena, however, he felt he had seen better.[53]

"Usually after five minutes I can tell if there is something special. We're hitting balls, and I'm going, 'these girls aren't that good'. There were arms and legs flying everywhere, beads flying out of their hair. They were improvising, hitting off their back feet", he recalled.[54]

If you watch any top level tennis player, professional or junior, their movement is often flawless. If you watch only the top half of their body during a point, they glide across the court in a way similar to a swan coasting through water. Novak Djokovic has mastered the art of movement. No matter what, his shots are never improvised. He makes sure he is balanced and his technique consistent when playing every shot. What Macci first saw was virtually the opposite of that; two young sisters playing pretty much all over the place.

What happened that day is very much a cautionary tale for all coaches. Never judge a book by its cover. First impressions can often be deceiving, and one shouldn't prejudge the value of something or someone in a hurry, and that rule certainly applies to tennis coaching. Whilst it's true the Williams sisters weren't as average as it first seemed, Macci hadn't witnessed them play points against one another yet. That was his next point of call, to watch them in a competitive setting, and what he saw next couldn't have been any different. "I swear to God, their stock went soaring through the hemisphere. Their footwork got better, their prep got better, they cleaned up their act. What blew me away was their burning desire to run and fight and get to every ball like their hair was on fire. I had never seen two kids try so hard. I had never seen bodies that could move like that", rejoiced Macci.[54] He knew right at that moment they could go on to transcend the game. They were both big and strong, and could produce power that other girls their age could not. Similar body types were found in other physical sports, but not tennis. With the right guidance and instruction, Macci knew he could achieve wonderful things with the pair. "I didn't think they could become number one and number two in the world. I knew they could right then", he preached.[53] From that day on, Richard Williams put his faith in Rick Macci to turn his two daughters from raw to ruthless, and that's exactly what he set out to do.

Grenelefe

Up until that moment, both Serena and Venus had been trained by their father. Rick Macci's new involvement in their development, however, meant a change of scenery. When their new coach invited the girls to train at his illustrious training academy in Grenelefe, Florida, the Williams family hastened to accept. The Rick Macci International Tennis Academy was to be their new training venue, and immediately, the trio began preparing for the future.[53]

Originally, whilst being tremendous athletes, the Williams sisters had a number of flaws in their game. They could hit the ball hard, but would often be off-balanced and clumsy. As seen previously, balance is paramount in tennis, and without it there's a glass ceiling that stops you from reaching new levels. Macci set out on ensuring his new students became even better athletes than they already were, and that started by encouraging them to play other sports in between practice sessions. Basketball, taekwondo, baseball, football, and even dancing became part of their daily routine, with each sport containing movement patterns and learning processes that can help improve tennis performance.[11] Learning to dance in particular was a fantastic way of teaching the girls how to keep their balance, strengthen their core, and help with coordination. Three fundamentals in the sport of tennis.

In regards to the other sports, Macci incorporated ball throwing into practice sessions. The girls were tasked with throwing baseballs and footballs to breed better motion when playing strokes, in particular the serve. There is evidence to indicate a positive transfer of learning between overhand throwing and the serve. Overarm throwing enables tennis players to produce a strong rotational movement in the shoulder, a movement crucial in generating high ball speed. Many students of the game often note how a good "throwing arm" gives a player a head start when it comes to prowess in the serve.[11] Whilst many other female players competed in one sport, the Williams sisters were using a wide variety of sports to improve their tennis, and this gave them an edge.[53]

Macci's unorthodox methods went beyond taking other sports and using them to improve tennis attributes. Whilst training in Grenelefe, the tennis courts were surrounded by a beautiful golf course. Unsurprisingly, Macci put the course to good use with the girls. Every day they were made to jog on the spot in the course's bunkers, with the sand making it much harder than it normally would have been on a normal surface.

With Richard Williams' blessing, Macci ensured training was always difficult. Rigorous practice routines would entail conditions far worse than they would experience on the pro tour once their days as a junior were over. The introduction of male training partners was a way of preparing the young girls for that eventuality. Boys a few years older than Serena would fire shots at double the speed any of her actual tournament opponents would have done, but she never complained. Her confidence certainly wasn't concealed when she competed at the academy. "In practice, all Serena did was play guys. She beat guys three to four years older than her. It didn't matter who was on the other side of the net. She didn't look at it like this girl is ranked this or that guy is sixteen. At eleven, she told me she thought she was better than John McEnroe". It may have been a tongue and cheek comment, but Serena, showing the confidence every athlete needs, really meant it, according to her coach.[54]

On the contrary, Venus didn't always win all of her practice matches at the academy against her older opponents. In a way similar to that of Toni Nadal, Macci saw it as a way to toughen Venus up. He, like Toni, wasn't a fan of building up a child's confidence to the point a defeat would destroy their self belief. He wanted his young students to lose, it meant making them stronger. "Venus didn't win a match at the academy. I let her play matches, and she didn't win a match for two years", he admitted.[53] It's hard to imagine any parent allowing that to happen in the world we live in today, hearing of their child lose practice matches every single time would probably send most parents crazy. Richard Williams didn't mind it, though.

So long as it was improving Venus' mentally, he was happy.[53]

The attribute that shone through in both girls at the time was their ambition. As Doris Goodwin writes in her book on leadership, "privilege can stunt ambition, just as lack of privilege can fire ambition".[6] Whilst the Williams' sisters weren't born into poverty, the family finances were stretched thin at various points in their childhood years. This may have been a reason for their fierce desire to be the best, to create a better life for not only themselves but for their families. Incredible drive is a trait found in every star player in any sport, and in the Williams sisters it was there in abundance from a young age.

After a couple of years training in Grenelefe, Macci decided to change the venue of his academy to Delray Beach, a small city on Florida's southeast coast. Without hesitation, the Williams family up sticks and relocated, showing loyalty and faith in their coach. Immediately, people took notice of the sisters in their new location. The scenery may have been different, but their training was very much the same. People would find themselves amazed at the amount of time Macci would spend with them out on court. Former Grand Slam winner Mary Pierce often stayed at the academy, and recalled witnessing the hard work all three of them put in. "I was living in an apartment on the third floor, and right below me were some clay courts", remembered Pierce. "They'd wake me up. I'd look out my window, and there they are: the Williams family. They were on the court all day long, from morning until night. All day, hitting balls and hitting balls and hitting balls".[55]

Despite being at a top academy with an array of beautiful courts of all surfaces, the sisters wouldn't always train on them. In another tactic similar to Toni Nadal using limp and lifeless tennis balls to ensure his nephew became accustomed to reacting to any situation, Macci had his own way of improving the girls. He would often take them, with their father, to a local tennis court not far from the facility, filled with large cracks and potholes. Not only was this to ground them, as the courts resembled similar ones used in their hometown of Compton, but it enabled them to react quickly to a wayward bounce or an uneven surface. It was another way of making sure practice sessions were harder than actual matches.

Up until that point, despite having played against boys and older opponents at the academy, the girls had limited experience of playing in actual tournaments against girls their age. As they grew from youngsters into teenagers, the desire to see them compete grew stronger.[53]

By the time the pair were ready to play in tournaments, the hard work that Macci had put into them was paying off. It should be said that their coach hasn't always taken the credit for their rise to greatness however, claiming genetics are a major factor in their tennis excellence. When the two would practice serving, it was Serena's serve that stood out as being better, even back then. Macci would practice the serve with them every single day, with the duo working on the same drills and routines. What separated Serena from her sister however, was her build. What Serena lacked in height she made up for in power. Macci confessed that Serena's genetics gave her a slight edge over Venus when it came to serving. "Her motion was a little more natural", he recalled when comparing the two. "She had a more natural shoulder turn. She was a little more rhythmic. Venus was a little more mechanical".[53]

It wasn't long before the Williams sisters took to the professional tour, and immediately changed the game of women's tennis forever. Their agility, power and technical efficiency saw them rise to fame before either of them had hit their twentieth birthday. For three and a half years the girls trained at the academy, learning their trade and preparing themselves for the pro tour. Rick Macci was the first professional coach that the girls ever had, and somebody who deserves a huge amount of credit for laying the foundation for the game each of the sisters developed.

Crisis Strikes

When Abigail Adams wrote to her son, John Quincy Adams, in the midst of the American Revolution, she suggested that good leaders come in times of crisis. "Great necessities call out great virtues" were her exact words.

When Serena Williams suffered defeat in the first round of the French Open in 2012, it was indeed labelled a crisis. Serena was a dominant force in the women's game by 2012, having already won 13 Grand Slam titles. Throughout her entire career, she had never tasted defeat in the first round of a Grand Slam, so it was no surprise that her loss to Virginie Razzano sent shock waves throughout the sport.

The match itself was fascinating. Ranked 111th in the world at the time, her French opponent was given little to no hope of recording a victory, with a routine win expected for Serena. The years of training against older, stronger and usually male players with Rick Macci had enabled Serena to develop short-term memory loss - the ability to continually look forward, never letting the previous point affect her confidence. It's a trait found in both Venus and Serena. They refuse to allow their head to drop. A bad shot is forgotten in an instant, and is usually followed by a marvelous one. A difficult set is brushed aside and learned from immediately. It's a scary trait to play against. Opponents know that snatching a game off them doesn't knock their confidence, it actually motivates them. It was therefore the style of Serena's first round defeat that made it all the more devastating.

After taking the first set 7-5, the second set went to a tie-breaker, where Serena eventually found herself 5-1 up, just two points away from victory. What happened next was the definition of the word "collapse". Razzano won six points in a row, and took the second set after a 7-5 win in the tie-breaker. After a couple of bad line calls, an usual amount of unforced errors, and an opponent with the French crowd behind her,

Serena fell apart. Despite saving seven match points, her usual bullet proof mentality seemed to vanish. She succumbed to Razzano 6-3 in the third and final set, and subsequently crashed out of the French Open. It was more than a shock result, it was an extremely humbling loss that forced Serena to assess her game. Her season hadn't been brilliant so far that year, and she had gone over a year without a Grand Slam, something unheard of since she became a professional.

Rather than fly home, Serena decided to stay in Paris, and flew to Patrick Mouratoglou's training academy situated in the French capital. In times of crisis in a player's career, they need a person strong enough to help turn it around. Somebody who can provide a much needed breath of fresh air: in Frenchman Mouratoglou, she found that.

Patrick Mouratoglou

"Leaders in every field need to know human nature, to know the needs of the human soul", wrote Theodore Roosevelt. Serena's new coach had suffered his fair share of setbacks in life, having been tempted out of a career in athletics by his father at an early age. He understood what frustration looked like, and it no doubt helped him grasp what Serena was going through when she arrived at his academy after her French Open defeat, searching for guidance on her game. When speaking to the press after her loss, Serena lamented at the amount of errors she made. "I just felt I couldn't get a ball in play. When I did, I just felt like I was hitting the ball late". The thing more peculiar than her unusual amount of unforced errors, which stood at 47 against Razzano, was her fragile mental state. "I did everything I needed to do to win, but mentally I fell apart. I came undone. I'm not sure why, but I just could not get it together", Serena confessed.[56] She let her mistakes eat away at her, which in turn diminished her confidence. It was completely unlike Serena, and Patrick Mouratoglou was tasked with helping the American regain her form. At the age of 30, Serena was still showing the ambition that had shone through in her days in Grenelefe. She wasn't content with 13 Grand Slam titles, and rather than settle for what she had achieved, she vowed to take her game to another level.

Upon arriving at Mouratoglou's academy, Serena was taken aback by his approach. He was known throughout the tour as being fiery and fearless, but the man she began working with that day was quite the opposite. He was sensitive, caring and open. As she hit with a couple of different players, Patrick watched closely, but at first wasn't prepared to offer any sort of guidance. He was assessing everything about Serena's game, from her footwork, to her strokes, to her attitude. Serena herself has confessed she was a little confused. She wanted to see him in action, to witness the man who had guided so many players to success almost instantly. "That first day I will never forget, because I don't remember him saying a single word". Neverthe-less, it was those few days with Mouratoglou that changed the course of her tennis career. "I don't remember what happened, or what Patrick said, but I do remember loving it", recalled Ser-ena on the first time she met with the Frenchman. "He sounded just like my dad. Confident in me, fearless and hungry".[56]

When it came time to leave, Serena was convinced she had found her new coach. He was innovative and confident in his work, and from that day on they worked with each other almost every single day. The first challenge the pair would face was Wimbledon, the following Grand Slam after her painful first round defeat at the French Open. At 30 years old her career was at a crossroads. She was a great tennis player, but not yet historic. That soon changed with her new French coach at the helm.

A Fresh Start

Academics who have studied the development of leaders have found that resilience, partnered with the ability to remain am-bitious when faced with adversity, is a key attribute when ex-amining potential leaders. More important than the adversity they faced, was the way in which they overcame their negative experiences to help mould their leadership skills.[6]

"When I arrived in the professional tennis world with innova-tive ideas, people thought that I was crazy, an idealist and a dreamer", confessed Mouratoglou.[57]

The Frenchman was somebody who had never left an impression on the game as a player, and up until the age of 26, had been groomed by his father to take over the family's renewable energy business, much to his dissatisfaction. He had battled illness as a child, and was the victim of bullying at school growing up. Despite finding joy in playing tennis, he had spent the majority of his life away from the game, under the orders of his parents. It was no surprise that when he embarked on a coaching career in the 1990s it was met with skepticism from those in the game, and even those closest to him. What could a man who had no prior experience achieve in the sport? Especially an element of the game as complex as tennis coaching. Throughout all the negativity, Mouratoglou didn't let anything affect his ambition to become a leading tennis coach, however. "My story with tennis started with a big frustration. But I always consider that frustration can be a huge motivator", he recalls.[57] His ability to look past his initial difficulties can be pinpointed to the immense confidence he has in himself. His self belief is a trait that helped him overcome his early frustrations, but it's a characteristic he has not just in himself, but in every player he coaches.

For Mouratoglou, as far as he is concerned, the player he is currently working with at the time is the best player in the world, a player who can accomplish anything. Whether it was youngsters like Gilles Muller or Marcos Baghdatis in the early 2000s, to Grand Slam champions like Serena Williams, the Frenchman has always permeated belief into his players.

Some people are able to extract wisdom from their own experiences, and others are not. Some people lose their bearings, whilst others come out the other side of adversity with greater resolve and purpose. Mouratoglou is the latter, and when he began working with Serena for the 2012 Wimbledon Championships, he vowed to use all his experience of adversity to connect with Serena. Serena's frustration with the way in which her career had stalled resonated with her new coach, and they immediately formed a unique bond.

Mouratoglou has stated there are two types of coaches: There are those who complain about their player, about their faults and shortcomings, and on the contrary, there are coaches who adapt and find solutions. It's common for a tennis coach to become frustrated their player isn't listening to them, but as far as Mouratoglou is concerned, it is the coach's job to make themselves heard.[56] Whenever one of his clients loses, the Frenchman immediately assesses the situation and looks for improvement. He never tries to blame or search for excuses, and he is more than happy to take the blame for a defeat. "Ever since the start of my career, I have always asked myself after my player has lost: What could I have done differently", he confessed. "Did my player fail to follow the tactics? Was my player in the right state to play? Was there an area of their game that failed them? Was the opponent able to exploit one of my player's weaknesses and if so how could we have avoided that? Where did I go wrong". By taking full responsibility for his players' defeat, Mouratoglou is able to find a solution and make progress.[56] It is rare for somebody in the Frenchman's position, particularly at such an elite level, to take on the burden of a defeat and subsequently shift the blame from player to coach. As we have seen in the pages prior however, coaches fit players in the way a key fits a lock. No two keys are the same, all with different edges and curves, and there is certainly no master key to tennis coaching. When Serena Williams started preparing for Wimbledon with her new coach, she soon realised she had found the key she had been looking for to unlock her greatness.

The Plan of Action

In a way similar to all leading tennis coaches, Patrick Mouratoglou came up with a plan to see his player become the best in the world once again. The events of his childhood and early coaching career had prepared Mouratoglou for this moment. Serena was a player he had a huge amount of respect for, and as always, he had no doubts he could guide her back to the number one spot in the rankings. Perhaps it was utter relief that caused Serena to forget exactly what was said that day when she arrived at his academy. She knew she liked what she heard, but the actual words seemed to get away from her.

It only took a few minutes for Patrick to figure out where she was going wrong. He explained to Serena how he had watched her match at the French Open, where she suffered that first round defeat, and that she was still making the same mistakes.

She had forgotten the core principles of playing tennis. "You're waiting for the ball to come to you rather than moving forward towards it", he explained. "When you hit the ball, you're not balanced. Your feet need to be further apart and your centre of gravity needs to be lower at the moment of contact with the ball to give you better stability".[56] The duo immediately started working on it, and straight away there were improvements. It's truly remarkable how it took Mouratoglou just a matter of minutes to spot a flaw in Serena's game. Spotting areas of improvement is simple in a player who is at the start of their tennis journey, but spotting a weakness so quickly in that of a 13 time Grand Slam champion, not so much.

Mouratoglou set out the following plan to ensure Serena was to earn her first Grand Slam in over a year:

I. Re-establish her confidence.

II. Deal with her stress.

III. Make her more efficient in matches.

IV. Rebuild a major weapon.

Breathing confidence into a player like Serena Williams looks a relatively easy task on paper. In 2012, despite not being in the best form, she was an icon in the sport of tennis. Having won every Grand Slam at least once, her standing in the game was huge, so surely confidence was never going to be an issue for a player who had achieved so much.

Like all top athletes in any sport however, confidence can escape you as quickly as it arrives. When preparing for Wimbledon, Mouratoglou knew he had to pick his words carefully. Serena had to see that her new coach had absolutely no doubts about her ability. "Behind the player who was going through a temporary moment of weakness I could still see the champion", he recalled. "At this precise moment of her career this was what she needed".[56]

Whilst letting Serena know verbally of his belief in her game, there were still improvements needed on the court. When a player is low on confidence, their game is often out of sorts. Hesitation can creep in. Strokes are more hesitant, and reactions not as fast. In order to combat this, the duo worked on the basics, as if she was back in Compton training with her father in the early 90s. Patrick focused on stability when hitting the ball, and encouraged Serena to move forward into her shots at the point of contact. By giving his American player more control and feel when striking, he knew it would in turn increase her confidence. The belief she gained was backed up by having a coach standing by her side who wholeheartedly believed in her.[56]

Serena had become so used to winning that failure to do so caused her immense stress. Being a professional tennis player is stressful enough. You are regularly travelling, and away from friends and family. You are constantly in different places, playing a variety of opponents, and the unknown can be a trigger for anxiety. If you add to that an unhealthy relationship with losing, it can quickly become too much for anybody to deal with. To overcome this and create a better environment, Mouratoglou set out to extend Serena's comfort zone. Whilst immersing yourself in activities you don't feel comfortable with can help you grow, it's just as important to live within familiar territory, particularly on the professional tour. To achieve this, Serena's new coach began to give her as much information on opponents as possible in pre-game meetings. "Even if Serena has already faced her opponent before, I endeavor Serena to help read her game better and to know more about how they act", stated her coach.[56] Allowing Serena to walk out on court with a clear idea of how her opponent was going to play offered her a sense of calm. Whether it was advice on where they were most likely to serve, or their tendency to hit down the line early on the backhand to avoid cross-court rallies - all this information helped Serena extend her comfort zone.[56]

What separates Mouratoglou from the other coaches mentioned in this book, is his immense organisational skills. After every match Serena plays, he keeps records of her opponent and sorts them into individual files. "I keep dozens of hours of recordings of each match played by every player on the circuit", said the French coach. This enables him to devise blueprints on how to beat almost anybody. Their strengths, weaknesses and general style of play are noted to remove any form of surprise for his players when they take to the court. His belief that tennis should be based on facts rather than opinion is a clear indication of his methods.[56]

To coincide with her on court work and guidance on op-ponents, the task of ensuring Serena became as efficient as possible during matches required another unique solution. How Serena plays in tournaments is often a result of her mental state. She has the ability to beat anybody on any given day, but the thing that makes her unbeatable is her frame of mind. When she is psychologically ready, her game is too. Mouratoglou is a firm believer that it is the responsibility of a coach to ensure their player walks on court in the best possible mental state. There are a number of people who believe that addressing the mental side of a players game is the job of a professional in the area, not that of a tennis coach. Certain coaches believe they are employed to improve the technical side of the game only, to make strokes look as beautiful as possible. But in Mouratoglou, Serena had a man who believed the psychological aspect of the sport was very much his problem to address. He doesn't believe in bringing in a psychologist to help boost a player's inner mind. "When I brief Serena on the day of a match, I tend to know exactly what her state of mind is", said Mouratoglou. "What I say is designed to put her into a state of excellence in the minutes before the start of a match".[56] If you look back at all the great leaders over the course of history, from Winston Churchill to Martin Luther King Jr, their ability to find the right words at the right moment was at the heart of their success. It is a difficult skill to develop, but Patrick knew his capacity for finding the right words could give Serena an edge when she stepped out on court, which in turn would improve efficiency in tournaments.

The final and perhaps most important area of Mouratoglou's plan to get Serena back to the top, was his decision to focus on her serve during practice. The fundamentals were all back in place. She was hitting the ball better, feeling more confident, and although she wasn't sure she'd bounce back from her French Open defeat and win Wimbledon, she felt better within herself. By freeing Serena of her tension, Patrick enabled his American student to rediscover her devastatingly brilliant serve. Throughout the previous year, she had struggled to hit the ball as hard when it came to her serve, and in turn it was negatively affecting her game. Being able to hold serve consistently would give Serena the chance to play with more freedom and risk when her opponent was serving. Throughout the lead up to Wimbledon, the former champion became engrossed with her ball throw, her swing, and her ability to fire her most powerful serves.

After only a month of working together, Serena and her new coach set off for the 2012 Wimbledon Championships.

*

The 14th Slam

For Patrick Mouratoglou and Serena Williams, their first Wimbledon journey was absolutely crucial for a number of reasons. Firstly, it was an opportunity to assess whether the work the Frenchman had done with Serena had worked, and failure to do so could put an early strain on the relationship. Secondly, despite being an excellent coach, Mouratoglou had never won a Grand Slam whilst in charge of a player, and he knew 2012 was a fantastic opportunity to do so.

The pair were still very much getting to know one another. How does Serena react when her shots aren't coming off? How does her coach react when his game plan isn't being meticulously followed? These were questions running through the minds of both player and coach when Serena began her first round match of the tournament against Poland's Barbora Strýcová.

As far as her coach was concerned, things started well. After winning her first round match, Serena's mental state seemed to have improved along with her serve. She brushed aside her opponent in straight sets and swiftly moved on to the next round. After winning her second and third round matches, the Serena Williams who had become such a prolific winner was starting to resurface. It was her fourth round match of the tournament however, that would cause far more issues.

Before the match, Serena had confided in her coach, admitting to feeling under the weather. In his usual form,

Mouratoglou prepped his player as best he could, and an unwell Serena took to Wimbledon's centre court, where she would face wild card Yaroslava Shvedova. The match proved far more difficult than both Serena or her coach would have liked. After breezing through the opening set 6-1, her opponent fought back tremendously, taking the second set 2-6. The final set could have gone either way. Serena didn't play particularly well, but in the end she came out victorious, meaning she qualified for the quarter-finals. In the recovery room after the match, her father seemed furious.

"What's happening to her?" he asked aggressively. Somewhat perplexed and angered in the way he had been spoken to, Mouratoglou replied, "I don't know". Nobody else knew that Serena wasn't feeling her best that day, and Patrick chose to keep it quiet. "You must know! You're the coach! I'll ask again: What's happening to her?"

Patrick Mouratoglou is a man who respects those he is speaking to, but somebody who expects that respect in return. He assertively told Richard Williams that he refused to be spoken to in such a way, explaining he was the right man for the job and that he would always take responsibility for his daughter's poor performances. Surprised by his brutal honesty, Serena's father stepped back. He knew at that moment the man guiding his daughter was the right one. He had tested Patrick, and with his reply, Mouratoglou showed exactly what he was made of.[56] From that day on, Richard Williams never disrespected him again. Perhaps that is why Serena had never had a full-time coach since she left Rick Macci. It could be a reasonable argument to suggest that no other coach has the inner toughness and confidence to stand up to Richard Williams like Mouratoglou did that day.

Despite the initial frustrations radiated by her father, Serena's victory over Shvedova had boosted her ranking to number five in the world standings. Thrilled, she sent a text message to her coach, explaining that no matter what happened for the rest of the tournament, she would keep her ranking of fifth. Showing the drive that helped him overcome his early setbacks, Mouratoglou wasn't impressed with his player. She was Serena Williams. A 13 time Grand Slam winner. The only place he expected her to be was the best player in the world, number five simply wasn't good enough. That same evening, Serena replied. She didn't understand how she had let herself become happy with a number five ranking. From there on out, it was to be "number one or nothing!"[56]

Her new found confidence, mixed with her improved serve and overall game, had catapulted Serena to the Wimbledon final. Mouratoglou had provided the American with invaluable tools that had proved the catalyst for her improved form. It had only been a month, but Serena had started to believe in her ability again. The match would be contested by herself and the number three seed, Agnieszka Radwańska. Serena's sister, Venus, had clinched the Wimbledon title on five occasions previously, and the younger of the two looked destined to equal that when she woke up that cool and cloudy morning. Throughout the tournament, Mouratoglou's impact had gradually increased. They were getting to know one another with each passing match, and as always, the French coach ensured Serena was in the best mental and physical shape possible. Identifying Radwańska's second serve as a potential area to exploit, he made sure his player was aware of her opponent's weakness.

From the get go, Serena was ruthless in her play. It wasn't that Radwańska was playing poorly, it was more Serena was playing with a fire in her belly, and a clear, concise game plan carefully thought out by her coach sitting in the players' box. Time after time, Serena annihilated her opponents second serve, showing no signs of forgiveness. Despite three of the opening four games going to deuce, the American possessed a cutting edge, taking all of the early games and racing into a 4-0 lead. The first set ended 6-1 to Serena, but perhaps to be expected, the final wasn't all smooth sailing. As we have seen, Serena's record in Grand Slams for a good couple of years wasn't up to her usual record breaking standards.

Whilst flying through the first set and a half, the second half of the match saw Serena overwhelmed with nerves. Had her comeback arrived too early? Did she require more time with Mouratoglou before aiming to win another Grand Slam? After losing the second set 5-7, a rain delay in the third and final set was exactly what she needed. A break in play gave Mouratoglou a chance to speak with his player. As fresh as their relationship was, all it took was a specific look from the

Frenchman to give Serena the encouragement she needed. "I knew that I would find the right words to make a difference", recalled Mouratoglou. "I also knew that when she looked me in the eyes during that short conversation, she would discover the reassurances and the confidence she needed in order to back out into battle even stronger".[56] Just like he knew he would, in those brief moments during the rain delay of that final, Mouratoglou had transferred the belief he had in himself to his player.

With Serena trailing 2-1 in the third set, the relentless effort that went into rediscovering Serena's serve became incredibly evident. In a flash, Serena fired four aces in a row, with each thunderbolt serve leaving Radwańska with no chance of return. Perhaps the most amazing stat of Serena's Wimbledon tournament that year was the fact she hit more aces than anybody else, male or female. With the gentleman's matches lasting longer due to a best of five format, her record of out serving everybody was amazing. She had rebuilt her major weapon in a big way, and it proved decisive in the final.

From that moment on, Serena ran riot. Radwańska, for all her effort, failed to win another game. Just 27 minutes after the rain delay, a thunderous backhand down the line rocketed past her opponent, and a jubilant Serena Williams fell to the floor. She had conquered her demons and emerged victorious for the fifth time on Wimbledon's centre stage. The plan that her coach had put in place a month earlier at the Mouratoglou Tennis Academy had worked to pinpoint perfection. Her confidence had been re-established, and she had coped with the stress in that final impeccably, with her head engrossed in the game plan. Her overall game had improved which made her more efficient, and of course Serena had proven once again that she was the best server of all time.

What happened that day was not the end of the Mouratoglou and Serena story. In fact, it was just the start. "I think it is definitely the beginning of something great", confessed Serena after the match, giving an inclination that she knew there was more to come with her new coach guiding her. Patrick himself knew the pair could achieve more, and immediately set out on doing so. "The tournament is over, and I know that from now onwards, beginning from tomorrow, I will refocus on new objectives". A very typical response from the Frenchman. Never satisfied. Always looking for that next victory. He had achieved his first Grand Slam as a coach, but he was far from content.

Mouratoglou has never envisaged himself as being a typical tennis coach. He has thought differently to others from the very beginning. From his methodical approach when analysing opponents using data, to his belief that the mental side of the game is within the realms of his job description. "My job consists of enabling my students to go beyond their limits, in order to make their dreams possible", confessed Mouratoglou.

Since their first meeting in 2012 after the French Open, Serena Williams has dominated women's tennis. In the eight years they have been working together, they have accumulated ten Grand Slam titles, and an Olympic gold medal. An astonishing record. Under Mouratoglou's care, Serena has gone from a leading women's tennis player to a historic superstar, whose name will forever be remembered in the sport. There are only a handful of coaches throughout history who have achieved success no matter what player they have worked with. To achieve such unprecedented success requires a skill set set that allows a coach to unlock a player's potential from a number of variables. From behaviour and personal relationships, to technical work and medical problems, Mouratoglou takes responsibility for every aspect of his player's game, and this is fundamentally what sets him apart.[56]

Patrick is lucky to have Serena, and Serena is lucky to have Patrick. Together however, they are simply unstoppable.

Table 5.1: Serena Williams Career Grand Slams by Year

1999	2002	2003	2005
U.S Open	U.S Open French Open Wimbledon	Australian Open Wimbledon	Australian Open

2007	2008	2009	2010
Australian Open	U.S. Open	Wimbledon Australian Open	Wimbledon Australian Open

2012	2013	2014	2015
Wimbledon U.S Open	French Open U.S. Open	U.S. Open	Australian Open French Open Wimbledon

2016	2017		
Wimbledon	Australian Open		

Chapter Six

6

The Future of Tennis Coaching

"You can have the nicest academy in the world, it doesn't make any difference, it's all about the people. Our job is all about the people".

Patrick Mouratoglou

THROUGHOUT THIS BOOK we have seen a number of attributes that make up a top coach. Interpersonal skills are vital, knowledge of the game imperative, and tactical wisdom a great separator. Perhaps the most important characteristic of any innovative coach, whether in tennis or any sport, is adaptability. The strength to adapt to new trends and directions.

Tennis coaching thirty years ago focused heavily on a blocked like system, with repetitive strokes repeated over and over. That's not to say this method doesn't work today, it does. Coaches still implement this style of training into a player's training regimen. Gradually, however, as seen with Gullikson and Sampras, coaching has advanced, with players training more openly and with more randomness. Toni Nadal's ability to ensure Rafa learned the game off his own accord was a major contributor in his meteoric rise to the top.

As we enter the year 2021, the future of tennis coaching may already be upon us, and it looks set to come through the use of data and statistics. When identifying what coaching looks like in other top sports in the modern day, analysing data to improve performance is at the forefront. The use of "expected goals" has been somewhat of a revelation in the sport of football, with every attack noted and examined to assess the probability of a goal. This in turn can help managers understand where their team is most efficient.[58]

If we translate that to the game of tennis, the most promising up and coming players are coached by individuals who wholeheartedly believe in the use of data to get the most out of their player. Twenty-year-old Canadian prodigy Felix Auger Aliassime and his coach Fred Fontang have worked with Tennis Analytics, a company who uses a data driven approach for analysing matches, for a number of years.

Perhaps the one coach who has been most vocal about his belief in this approach is Patrick Mouratoglou. As we have seen, the Frenchman has kept his own data on players for a while, showing signs he was ahead of the curve. When speaking on the matter, Mouratoglou has always been very open about his opinion on the trend. "The use of multiple cameras, in combination with the use of relevant statistics can give you an understanding about the trajectory of balls, about the contact point or about different areas of the court", he explained.[56]

Whilst relentless on court training will always be a fundamental part of tennis coaching, the increased use of technology in the game will allow coaches to possess a thorough and complete analysis of a player that wouldn't have been possible a decade ago. Coaches who have adapted and embraced the new phenomenon appear to be getting a head start, with Mouratoglou a case in point. Change can be daunting, but it may become paramount to stay relevant in the category of elite tennis coaching.

The use of on court coaching has also become a topic of debate amongst those in the professional circuit. There appears to be stalemate in regards to the two ways of thinking; does the sport remain loyal to its roots and continue to conform to the rules put in place decades ago, or is a modern and more progressive way of thinking beneficial for the game to move forwards.

Coaching is imperative in every single sport, and without passionate tennis coaches, the game wouldn't be the same. In some ways however, lawmakers have portrayed tennis coaching in a negative light when it comes to in game guidance. Whether it's football, boxing, basketball, or the majority of other sports, the coach or coaching team are just as visible as the players themselves. A football manager's technical area is as close to the pitch as you can get without actually being on it. Watching Rafa Benitez squeeze his hands together to inform his team to be more compact is seen as genius. In contrast, any sign of a tennis coach offering their player guidance whilst playing a match is seen as the ultimate sin. It's strange really, and questions do need to be asked as to whether such a rule is necessary.

Those against a changing of the laws argue tennis is a one on one sport, where a player should be left to figure out problems on their own. They may have a point, but tennis is a form of entertainment for millions around the world. Wouldn't it be great to see Marian Vajda or Patrick Mouratoglou on the side of the court helping their respective players. Offering fans the chance to see their work in full view could not only entertain, but inspire. Whilst there have been experiments, most notably in the women's game, the next step could be for the enabling of tennis coaches to sit court side during a Grand Slam, something that could take tennis coaching to another level.

All of the above ideas on what tennis may look like in years to come are as exciting as they are fascinating. Above all, however, whether you are a player, coach, or simply a fan, the future of the game looks compelling. All of the coaches mentioned in this book have left their footprint on the game, and their achievements will in no doubt stand the test of time. As those who have come before us as inspiration, we can safely look forward with great optimism to the next generation of leading tennis coaches, wherever they are and whoever they may be.

Bibliography

[1]   Fred Simonsson. *How Tennis Has Evolved Over The Years*. URL: https : / / tennispredict.com/?s=how+tennis+has+evolved.

[2]   N. Koran. *The Zen of Tennis: A Winning Way of Life*. Nancy Koran, 2002. ISBN: 9780967979694.

[3]   Laurie. *The Match That Changed Tennis*. 2012. URL: https : / / www . laurietennisarticles.net/2012/12/the-match-that-changed-tennis_10.html.

[4]   Pete Sampras and Peter Bodo. *A Champion's Mind: Lessons from a Life in Tennis*. Three Rivers Press, 2009. ISBN: 978-03-0738-330-3.

[5]   Kevin Palmer. *Pat Rafter names Pete Sampras his toughest opponent and lifts lid on 'cry baby' comment*. 2020. URL: https://www.tennis365.com/atp-tour/pat-rafter-names-pete-sampras-his-toughest-opponent-and-lifts-lid-on-cry-baby-comment/.

[6]   D.K. Goodwin. *Leadership: In Turbulent Times*. Simon & Schuster, 2019. ISBN: 9781476795935.

[7]   Robin Finn. *Tim Gullikson, 44, Tennis Coach and Player*. 1996. URL: https:// www.nytimes.com/1996/05/04/sports/tim-gullikson-44-tennis-coach-and-player.html.

Bibliography

[8]   James Buddell. *Pete Sampras - The Making Of A Champion*. 2010. URL: https://www.atptour.com/en/news/deuce-us-open-2010-sampras.

[9]   David Higdon. *Timmy, from Higgy*. 1996. URL: https://www.tennisserver.com/netgame/netgame_5_11_96.html.

[10] Peter Mendelsohn. *Tearful Determination – How Pete Sampras battled through his darkest moment*. 2017. URL: http://tennisdork.com/pete-sampras/.

[11] B. Elliott, M. Reid, and M. Crespo. *Tennis Science: How Player and Racket Work Together*. University of Chicago Press, 2015. ISBN: 9780226136400.

[12] Brain Game Tennis. *Men Rally Length: 2016 - 18 RG vs. US Open*. URL: https://www.braingametennis.com/dirtballer/men-rg-vs-us-open-rally-length/.

[13] J. Connors and R.J. LaMarche. *Jimmy Connors, how to Play Tougher Tennis*. A tennis magazine book. Golf Digest/Tennis, 1986. ISBN: 9780914178781.

[14] The Dallas Morning News. *Sampras always remembers coach who changed his life*. 2002. URL: http://www.samprasfanz.com/news/x2005news/020718.html.

[15] Kevin Palmer. *Pete Sampras in quotes, featuring brutal Andre Agassi blast*. 2018. URL: https://www.tennis365.com/tennis-legends/pete-sampras-in-quotes-featuring-brutal-andre-agassi-blast/.

[16] R.E. Neustadt. *Presidential Power and the Modern Presidents: The Politics of Leadership from Roosevelt to Reagan*. Free Press, 1991. ISBN: 9780029227961.

[17] R. Stauffer. *The Roger Federer Story: Quest for Perfection*. New Chapter Press, 2007. ISBN: 9780942257397.

[18] C. Bowers. *Roger Federer: The Greatest: The Greatest*. John Blake, 2011. ISBN: 9781843585923.

[19] Marko Trninić, Vladan Papić, and Viktorija Trninić. "Influence of coach's leadership behaviour and process of training on performance and competition efficacy in elite sport." In: *Acta Kinesiologica* 3 (Jan. 2009).

[20] T. Kajtna et al. *Trener: športna psihologija in trenerji*. Fakulteta za šport, Inštitut za šport, 2007. ISBN: 9789616583237.

[21] David Law. *Federer Come of Age*. URL: https://www.thetennispodcast.net/blog/2020/7/6/federer-comes-of-age-2001.

[22] Crystal Wu. *Flourishing for Sports*. Partridge Singapore, 2014.

[23]   Uche Amako. *Roger Federer: Pundit reveals amazing story of what ex-coach Peter Lundgren said of Swiss*. URL: https://www.express.co.uk/sport/tennis/1098326/Roger-Federer-Peter-Lundgren-Daniela-Hantuchova-Indian-Wells-BNP-Paribas-Open.

[24]   CNN. *Federer splits from coach Lundgren*. URL: http://edition.cnn.com/2003/SPORT/12/09/tennis.federer/.

[25]   P. Bodo. *Roger Federer: The Man, The Matches, The Rivals*. Diversion Books, 2012. ISBN: 9781938120398.

[26]   Nottingham Trent University. "Adversity in personal lives helps athletes thrive under pressure, study shows." In: (). URL: https://www.ntu.ac.uk/about-us/news/news-articles/2017/07/adversity-personal-lives-helps-athletes-thrive-under-pressure.

[27]   L.J. Wertheim. *Strokes of Genius: Federer, Nadal, and the Greatest Match Ever Played*. Houghton Mifflin Harcourt, 2009. ISBN: 9780547232805.

[28]   R. Nadal and J. Carlin. *Rafa: My Story*. Little, Brown Book Group, 2011. ISBN: 9780748129454.

[29]   T. Nadal. *Todo se puede entrenar*. Alienta, 2015. ISBN: 9788416253081.

[30]   Toni Nadal. *Online Courses for Tennis Coaches*. URL: https://www.world-mastery.com/artist/toni-nadal.

[31]   Richard Pagliaro. *Training With Toni Nadal in Costa Mujeres*. URL: https://www.tennisnow.com/News/2020/March/Training-with-Toni-Nadal-in-Costa-Mujeres.aspx.

[32]   Jovica Ilic. *Rafael Nadal Unveils The Best Decision He Made In Career*. URL: https://www.tennisworldusa.org/tennis/news/Rafael_Nadal/82286/rafael-nadal-unveils-the-best-decision-he-made-in-a-career/.

[33]   Peter Bodo. *Should we be celebrating Rafael Nadal's split with Uncle Toni?* URL: https://www.espn.co.uk/tennis/story/_/id/18677750/tennis-celebrating-rafael-nadal-split-uncle-toni.

[34]   The Guardian. *Nadal through after Djokovic injury*. URL: https://www.theguardian.com/sport/2006/jun/07/tennis.frenchopen2006.

[35]   Mark Meadows. *Interview-Tennis-Djokovic's ex-coach expected Serb's rise*. URL: https://www.reuters.com/article/tennis-open-piatti-idUKLDE74P2BH20110526?edition-redirect=uk.

Bibliography

[36]   C. Bowers. *The Sporting Statesman - Novak Djokovic and the Rise of Serbia*. Kings Road Publishing, 2014. ISBN: 1784180483.

[37]   Pro Tennis Network. *Marian Vajda*. URL: https://www.mytennisprofile.com/marian-vajda.

[38]   Uche Amako. *Novak Djokovic's coach Marian Vajda recalls the moment he decided to work with Serbian ace*. URL: https://www.express.co.uk/sport/tennis/1259856/Novak-Djokovic-coach-Marian-Vajda-Grand-Slams.

[39]   Christopher Clarey. *Youth Coach Helped Djokovic Fulfill Many of His Hopes*. URL: https://www.nytimes.com/2013/06/03/sports/tennis/03iht-coach03.html.

[40]   Daniel Hedley. *Roger Federer has never retired from a match in his professional career*. URL: https://www.givemesport.com/1541968-roger-federer-has-never-retired-from-a-match-in-his-professional-career.

[41]   Martyn Herman. *Nadal returns in unfamiliar role of underdog*. URL: https://www.reuters.com/article/uk-tennis-finals-nadal/nadal-returns-in-unfamiliar-role-of-underdog-idUKTRE7AI0OQ20111119.

[42]   Daniel Gould et al. "A Survey of mental skills training knowledge, opinions, and practices of junior tennis coaches." In: *Journal of Applied Sport Psychology* 11.1 (1999). DOI: 10.1080/10413209908402949.

[43]   N. Djokovic and W. Davis. *Serve to Win: The 14-Day Gluten-Free Plan for Physical and Mental Excellence*. Random House Publishing Group, 2013. ISBN: 9780345548993.

[44]   Bhargav Hazarika. *Coach Vajda explains how Novak Djokovic changed his game to beat Nadal at RG*. URL: https://www.sportskeeda.com/tennis/news-novak-djokovic-s-coach-explains-how-he-changed-his-game-to-beat-nadal-at-rg.

[45]   Kuchal. *'Djokovic forced to eat fish'- Marian Vajda*. URL: https://www.essentiallysports.com/djokovic-forced-to-eat-fish/.

[46]   Jeremy Sheppard and Warren Young. "Agility Literature Review: Classifications, Training and Testing." In: *Journal of sports sciences* 24 (Oct. 2006). DOI: 10.1080/02640410500457109.

[47]   BMJ. *Novak Djokovic shares his sportsmedicine secrets for success*. URL: https://blogs.bmj.com/bjsm/2014/06/28/secrets-to-success-interview-with-tennis-star-novak-djokkovic/.

[48]   Bhargav Hazarika. *I had doubts whether 'nervous' Novak Djokovic could win Roland Garros: Marian Vajda.* URL: https://www.sportskeeda.com/tennis/news-i-had-doubts-whether-nervous-novak-djokovic-could-win-roland-garros-marian-vajda.

[49]   Peter Gilbert. *Novak Djokovic splits with entire coaching team.* URL: https://www.skysports.com/tennis/news/12110/10863988/novak-djokovic-splits-with-entire-coaching-team.

[50]   Piers Newbery. *Australian Open: Novak Djokovic beaten by Chung Hyeon.* URL: https://www.bbc.co.uk/sport/tennis/42773242.

[51]   Christopher Clarey. *Novak Djokovic Reunites With an Old Coach and Rediscovers His Game.* URL: https://www.nytimes.com/2018/06/03/sports/novak-djokovic-french-open-coach.html.

[52]   Sampaolo. *Marian Vajda is named ATP Coach of 2018.* URL: https://www.ubitennis.net/2018/12/marian-vajda-named-atp-coach-2018/.

[53]   M.L. Corbett. *Serena Williams: Tennis Champion, Sports Legend, and Cultural Heroine.* Rowman & Littlefield Publishers, 2020. ISBN: 9781538109670.

[54]   Alyssa Roenigk. *Road to 23: The story of Serena's path to greatness.* URL: https://www.espn.com/espnw/culture/feature/story/_/id/17494146/road-23-story-serena-path-greatness.

[55]   Ben Rothenberg. *Returning to the Top, but With a New View.* URL: https://www.nytimes.com/2012/10/27/sports/tennis/serena-williams-back-on-the-rise-with-newfound-appreciation.html.

[56]   P. Mouratoglou and S. Williams. *The Coach.* Wymer Publishing, 2017. ISBN: 9781908724755.

[57]   Paul Fein. *The man who changed Serena.* URL: http://tennisconfidential.com/The_Man-Who_Changed_Serena.php.

[58]   J. Tippett. *The Expected Goals Philosophy: A Game-Changing Way of Analysing Football.* Independently Published, 2019. ISBN: 9781089883180.

Printed in Great Britain
by Amazon